MISTAKEN IDENTITY

Taking the Gospel to Heart

MATT BRINKLEY

Scripture taken from the Holy Bible, NEW INTERNATIONAL VERSION® Copyright © 1973, 1978, 1984 International Bible Society. All rights reserved throughout the world. Used by permission of International Bible Society.

Copyright © 2012 by Matt Brinkley Ministry, 560 Woodline Court, Roswell, GA 30076 All right reserved.

Cover Design, Layout and Production by Walt Wooden.

All material within this packet is Copyright material and may only be duplicated by permission from the author. You may contact the author at pact@pactministry.org Thank you!

Biography

Matt Brinkley's ministry experience spans over 37 years. He is a graduate of Covenant College (BS) and New Orleans Baptist Theological Seminary (ADiv). He was the founder and director of the Fellowship of Christian Students (1979-1983) in Macon, GA, served as Director of Ministries for Reach Out Ministries in Atlanta, GA (1985-1986), and then served as student pastor in Montgomery, Alabama at Trinity Presbyterian Church. In 1991 he moved to Atlanta to serve as student pastor at Perimeter Church (PCA). Eleven years later, Matt's responsibilities there broadened to include leadership over the Nextgen Division, and oversight of all ministries related to children and youth. In 2006 he went on staff at The Vine Community Church (PCA) serving as the Nextgen director and the oversight of adult discipleship.

Matt is the founder and director of PACT Ministry which was incorporated in 1996 to serve and encourage youth pastors in their personal walk with God, family life, and strategic ministry.

He is an active certified coach and facilitator/trainer for RightPATH Resources impacting leaders in Fortune 500 companies as well as executives running medium and small businesses.

Today, Matt splits his time between PACT and his responsibilities at the church. He has a great heart for God, exudes an honest and refreshing demeanor, and loves being with, understanding, and ministering to people.

In addition to this book, he is an author who has written three books (*Stay the Course*, *FOUR* and *Dating by the Book*), along with five discipleship manuals. He is a sought-after speaker for retreats and conferences.

Matt and his wife Vickie have three grown children. Matt Jr. (31), Andrew (27) and Mary Beth (24), and one incredible grandbaby, Nathan.

Special Thanks

Walt Wooden for the timeless commitment to create the layout and cover for the book.

Lisa Goddard for the dedicated grammatical editing.

Dedication

I would like to dedicate this book to the host of people that have invested untold hours over the years loving me, praying for me, being patient with me, challenging me, and living out dependence upon Christ in front of me. Thank you for the constant message to trust in Christ alone and helping me better understand what that means.

Table of Contents

Preface 8
Foreword: Christ alone Sanctifies 9
Introduction 14
Gus The Goose 16
Chapter 1 Ready to Jump! 18
Chapter 2 The Root of the Problem 23
Chapter 3 The Fleshly Spin of Despair 31
      Personal Reflections 1 33
      Personal Reflections 2 35
      Personal Reflections 3 37
Chapter 4 The Fleshly Spin of Despair (Part 2) 39
      Personal Reflections 4 41
      Personal Reflections 5 44
      Personal Reflections 6 46
Chapter 5 Fleshly Foundational Beliefs 48
      Personal Reflections 7 55

Table of Contents

Chapter 6 The Flesh…a Formidable Foe! 57

Chapter 7 Core Messages 63

        Core Messages Worksheet 70

Chapter 8 The Power of the Cross! 74

        Promises of the Cross Worksheet 85

Chapter 9 The Power of the Cross! (Part 2) 87

Chapter 10 Putting it All Together 97

        Impact from the Promises of the Cross Worksheet . 100

        Take the Gospel to Heart Worksheet 105

Chapter 11 Intimacy…The Spiritual Fuel for the Heart 106

Chapter 12 It's even Better! 119

Appendix 1 Whatever Happened to Ginny and Cory? 129

Case Study 1 Ginny 130

Case Study 2 Cory 138

Notes 146

Preface

You have just discovered a great book for either the individual reader or a small group. "Mistaken Identity" is sure to bless and deepen every believer's faith! In a fresh and creative way, this book takes the Christian reader on an eye-opening and life giving journey to discover their incredible identity in Christ. It guides each believer along a pathway that exposes nagging idols and then leads them to triumph through the power found in Christ alone.

To do this the author utilizes three things: 1) The incredible transforming truth of God's word; 2) A pathway of thinking that is practical and proven; 3) A real life storyline that the reader can identify with and apply. This journey is sure to be Christ-centered, enlightening, fruitful, and relationally rewarding.

This book is ideal for a small group experience. While the individual believer is encouraged to read this book, it is highly recommend that this study be done along with a small group who are willing to dive in together with a commitment to be prayerful, authentic, and expectant. Throughout the study there are very helpful questions to help the reader digest and apply the powerful life-giving principles shared.

The riches of Christ are indeed indescribable. Come discover and enjoy your rich inheritance in Christ as you journey through this exciting book.

May Christ bless each reader immeasurably beyond what they could ask or imagine throughout the journey!

Foreword:
Christ alone Sanctifies!

This book demands a proper set-up. The foreword is intended to give the reader strong footing as they enter into what I pray will be an encounter with our great God and a life-changing experience. It is from the vantage point shared in the forward that I fasten my hope…Christ alone for salvation and sanctification. Of course the grip by which I hold Him tightens and loosens, but His grip on me never falters. As you will see in the following testimony, it took a while for me to grasp the power of the gospel related to daily spiritual growth (sanctification). Since that time, I continue to marvel and grow in my depth and understanding of just how comprehensive and supernaturally transforming is the work of Christ. For some the testimony will simply be a reminder of where they have already been. For others it might be incredible new hope and new Biblical insight to greater understanding of the power of the gospel. It was for me. It is with thankfulness and joy that I introduce myself to you in this testimony knowing one hope… Christ alone.

The Backdrop:

It was in 1972 at the age of 17 that I met Christ as my Lord and Savior. I can vividly remember His unbelievable work in my life. The new sense of peace, joy, and freedom was literally overwhelming. All I could think about was what I needed to do next to get more of it. And that is exactly what I did. I set out to live the Christian life.

Saved by Grace/ Sanctification by Works?

No doubt those around me meant well, but rather than nurture the state of dependence in Christ that brought salvation, the instruction I received to spiritually grow seemed geared to self-action. And that I was good at. As fervently as I had pursued self-gratification before turning my life over to Christ, I now pursued spiritual gratification. Rather than the "means of grace" (Bible study, prayer, scripture memory, worship) serving to lead me down a pathway of utter dependence in Christ, I made them steps and disciplines to further my position with Christ. It is amazing how I am able to make everything about me. At first there was a sense of fulfillment. I was doing new things… and doing them better daily. But it wasn't long before I realized that something was very wrong. The things I wanted to do, I did not do… and the things I did not want to do, I did. But being persistent and determined… and knowing nothing different, I fought like a madman. Yes, I was a believer. I completely trusted Christ for everlasting life. When it came to spiritual growth, I was a madman like I was before I was a believer, but now simply on a religious chase with a new challenge and new goal… to live like the Christian that my Bible talked about.

Galatians 3:1- 5

You foolish Galatians! Who has bewitched you? Before your very eyes Jesus Christ was clearly crucified. I would like to learn just one thing from you. Did you receive the Spirit by observing the law, or by believing what you heard? Are you so foolish? After beginning with the Spirit, are you now trying to attain your goal by human effort? Have you suffered so much for nothing, if it really was for nothing? Does God give you His Spirit and work miracles among you because you observe the law, or because you believe what you've heard?

Please don't misunderstand my initial motivation. I genuinely had every intention to live for Christ's glory… the problem was, I didn't understand how this was attained. So I just tried harder, but the harder I tried, the higher the bar seemed to rise. Seemingly as soon as I took several steps forward, I would take a giant step backward, erasing all progress. The goals seemed to grow more complex as I studied His word. What initially felt like outward actions that needed correction (which I seemed to be accomplishing) became deep inner motives that I knew I couldn't correct. I was a mess… and only getting worse. I was defeated, frustrated, guilty, and hopeless. The finish line had disappeared into the distance. I was at the end of myself. I knew that God was for real! I never doubted that. But something was wrong with me. Who would rescue me? Or was it just hopeless?

I was overwhelmed! I had no other answers! It took 12 years to get to this point. It was at this time that our great God used a well-positioned friend to speak into my life. As I unfolded my painful testimony of defeat and assurance that I had no new answers or ideas, God used my friend to share simple truth with great power. Secrets were being revealed… or at least it felt that way to me. I discovered that a lack of knowledge and spiritual exuberance had swiftly led me away from the true source of my hope. Rather than to remain (John 15) in Him in a position of utter dependence, I sought to live for Him in my own strength. After genuinely receiving the gift of salvation in a broken and contrite manner, I quickly began to depend upon my flesh effort to serve Him. Practically speaking, I had abandoned the restorative power of the cross. I quickly traded it in for something much more familiar… performance. The cross is intended to restore the privilege to commune and utterly depend upon the creator. I had resorted to my own strength. I found myself estimating my accessibility to God and His happiness with me based upon my level of performance. Nobody had to teach me this… it all came naturally. It was the old nature bullying me.

I found myself with no answers and in despair. I was more aware of my depravity than ever. Had I spiritually run ashore or was defeat leading me into a deeper understanding of His great work in my life?

The Promise of Sanctification:

Until that day when I met with my friend, I did not understand that brokenness leading to utter dependence in Christ alone was the healthy mindset that engaged the supernatural empowerment of Christ. The same grace that saved me was the same grace that would sanctify (spiritually grow) me. In other words, Christ alone would accomplish the sanctifying work in me.

I Thessalonians 5: 23 clearly states this…"*May God Himself, the God of peace, sanctify you through and through. May your whole spirit, soul and body be kept blameless at the coming of our Lord Jesus Christ.*"

There are two types of sanctification talked about in scripture. One is positional sanctification: (I Corinthians 1: 12) at salvation, through Christ, the believer is set apart by the Holy Spirit with ascribed (imputed) righteousness and life. The other is progressive sanctification: (I Thessalonians 5: 23) the continued promised work of Christ through the Holy Spirit in the believer which sets him apart for God in his experience. This sanctification brings daily spiritual transformation, eliminating sins and producing Christ's fruit. Both are vital to the believer, but progressive sanctification is what I am referring to in this testimony. We must depend on Christ for our sanctification!

The question remains: If I completely trust Christ with my sanctification, what is my responsibility in the sanctification process? Colossians 2: 6 granted new perspective… "*So then, just as you received Christ Jesus as Lord, continue to live in him.*" According to this passage, if I could go back to my responsibility when I initially received Christ, I could find the answer to how to live for Him… or did it say "in Him."

When I accepted Christ I was desperate. Another way to put it is broken. Really broken… spiritually dead. I had nothing to offer. Christ was completely responsible for my salvation (Eph. 2: 8, 9). Even the faith by which I responded came from him (Romans 10: 17). We see brokenness communicated all through scripture. It is the constant in God's message to His people. (Isaiah 12: 2; Psalm 147:10-14; Psalm 5: 7; Proverbs 3: 5, 6)

According to Colossians 2: 6 I must stay in this state of brokenness to grow spiritually **(I Cor. 8: 6)**. The apostle Paul shares this imperative understanding of brokenness (weakness) throughout his writings, but particularly to the Church of Corinth. In II Corinthians 12: 9 he says… "*But he said to me, My grace is sufficient for you, for my power is made perfect in weakness.*" Therefore I will boast all the more gladly about my weaknesses, so that Christ's power may rest on me." Brokenness is the absolute assurance that our flesh has no capacity or competence to produce Godly results. (John 6: 62 – 64; Rom. 7: 18; Gal. 5: 19)

So who does? Only Christ! It was true at salvation and it remains true for sanctification. The believer's brokenness leads to dependence upon Christ alone. This is what broken people do. They depend! That is why it is integral to our faith. Broken people are dependent and dependent people cling. Christians cling to Christ who is their hope.

It is God's delight and passion to relate with His children. It is for God's glory that He demonstrates this love so thoroughly and extravagantly. Throughout John 15, as well as the whole Bible, God's message is a message of relationship. The centerpiece is Christ. The command is that Christ might dwell (abide) in our hearts. To abide is to take residence and relate.

Remaining in Him is to continue in a state of relationship and absolute trust in Christ... not only what he did to initially save you, but what he promises to do to sanctify you (Philippians 1: 6) God delights when we are in this position of absolute dependence… when our trust and faith is solely on Him. A Swiss theologian, Frederic Godet, defines this position of abiding as… "It is the continuous act by which the Christian lays aside all he might draw from his own wisdom, strength and merit, to desire all from Christ by the inward aspiration of faith."

So what do I do? Cling to Christ. Depend upon Him. Remember you are broken and needy. Sanctification is the process of realizing our insufficiency and Christ's sufficiency. We are responsible to remain in a state of brokenness and dependency upon Him. Even that is dependent upon Him. If you sense you have taken over, which we often do, invite Christ to bring you back to that place of need. Progressive sanctification is indeed a process. The believer's faith is in perpetual motion moving between Christ (brokenness, dependency, clinging to Christ) and self (pride, independence, clinging to the world). But God is faithful even when we are not. With His love and discipline, he continues to compel us throughout the sanctification process bringing us closer to dependence in Him alone (II Cor. 5: 14; Hebrew 12: 6). Just like my hope for salvation, my hope for sanctification is in Christ alone. Except for His great work, I realized I was completely helpless. What seemed like defeat for me simply led me back to where I began when I received Christ… dependent upon Him.

That day I cried out with a new prayer:

Father… Thank you for the work of Christ that gives me the privilege to be one with you and know you intimately. Lord, make that my primary motivation. Give me constant awareness of my inadequacy and faith to trust your sufficiency. May I live abundantly overflowing with your love and power! Because of the work of Christ, I come into your throne room just as I am. I confess that I am without means in my flesh to do any of this. But I know the work of Christ will deliver me. I can't do it… but you can! You indeed are faithful.

Introduction

"Spiritual victory"… now there's an interesting concept. I think that most believers would say they desire it. The apostle Paul did. He said… *"I have fought the good fight, I have finished the race, I have kept the faith. ⁸Now there is in store for me the crown of righteousness, which the Lord, the righteous Judge, will award to me on that day–and not only to me, but also to all who have longed for His appearing."* (II Tim. 4: 7 – 8) Paul clearly sensed spiritual victory in his life.

But what is spiritual victory? What did he mean to fight the fight, finish the race and keep the faith? In the American church culture we think of spiritual victory as living with a sense of harmony with God and in other primary relationships, with little spiritual warfare or major temptation, having our physical and emotional needs cared for (according to our definition of "cared for"), feeling productive, and experiencing no major crisis. This is a great definition of abundant blessings and there is certainly nothing wrong with seasons of life like this. However, I am afraid we confuse our blessings with spiritual victory. Is this what Paul was talking about when he exclaimed victory?

It is always important to read God's word in context. Prior to Paul's exclamation of spiritual victory he says in II Timothy 4: 6… *"For I am already being poured out like a drink offering",* which means that his life is a sacrifice. Being poured out as a sacrifice certainly isn't experiencing worldly comforts. To Paul, spiritual victory cannot mean simply having worldly comfort. Neither his life nor his words communicate that.

In Philippians 4: 12 – 13 he says… *"I know what it is to be in need, and I know what it is to have plenty. I have learned the secret of being content in any and every situation, whether well fed or hungry, whether living in plenty or in want. I can do everything through Him who gives me strength."* Note that Paul makes no apology for having times of worldly comfort. I am quite sure he was thankful for those respites. But his definition of victory had nothing to do with circumstances. For him it was much deeper. Spiritual victory was about Christ Jesus, the source of victory. His message was centered on knowing Christ. It seems that intimacy and companionship with Christ Jesus was victory.

*"Let us fix our eyes on Jesus, the **author** and **perfecter** of our faith, who for the joy set before Him endured the cross, scorning its shame, and sat down at the right hand of the throne of God."* Hebrews 12:2

"⁷But whatever was to my profit I now consider loss for the sake of Christ. ⁸What is more, I consider everything a loss compared to the surpassing greatness of knowing Christ Jesus my Lord, for whose sake I have lost all things. I consider them rubbish, that I may gain Christ ⁹and be found in Him, not having a righteousness of my own that comes from the law, but that which is through faith in Christ—the righteousness that comes from God and is by faith." Philippians 3: 7 – 9

Imagine knowing that kind of intimacy with Christ. Imagine knowing that level of love, acceptance, power, and security found only in Him. Imagine the kind of confidence that Paul had… not one based upon circumstances at all, but built upon security and promise that came through his relationship with Christ. Imagine what life would look like if we experienced true love, peace, freedom, and significance. Imagine the impact through our lives if Christ was that real to us. Christ came to meet us at our deepest level of need. He came to "do life" with us. He came to love us. He came to set us free.

If you, like I, have mistaken spiritual victory with anything less than this, it is time for us to raise our sights… to recalibrate… to look at our compass with a different goal in mind. Jesus Christ is ready to escort us on this journey. This journey will take us far beyond what we currently experience. It will take the believer beyond mere worldly comfort and temporary peace of mind. It is promised and He who promises is always faithful. This journey is sure to be rich in ways unimagined!

"¹⁹and to know this love that surpasses knowledge—that you may be filled to the measure of all the fullness of God. ²⁰Now to him who is able to do immeasurably more than all we ask or imagine, according to his power that is at work within us, ²¹to Him be glory in the church and in Christ Jesus throughout all generations, for ever and ever! Amen." Ephesians 3:19-21

³His divine power has given us everything we need for life and godliness through our knowledge of him who called us by His own glory and goodness. ⁴Through these He has given us his very great and precious promises, so that through them you may participate in the divine nature and escape the corruption in the world caused by evil desires." II Peter 1: 3, 4

The following is a lighthearted story to introduce the heart of this book.

Join me as we seek to Take the Gospel to Heart on the Pathway to Victory!

Gus The Goose

Gus met us at the door of the little cabin. His friendly and excited demeanor thrilled my children. Steve, the director of the camp where I was speaking, had instructed us to make ourselves at home in the quaint cabin and then meet him at the dining hall. We were not forewarned about the hospitality we would receive upon arrival. As I opened the squeaky door of the screened porch, Gus entered quickly as if to make sure everything was in order. He had obviously done this before. He quietly sat down on the porch as we moved our luggage inside. As my wife and I prepared to go to dinner, the children were sitting on the porch with Gus, completely preoccupied. There was something special about Gus that would entertain anyone. The family headed to the door of the cabin to go to dinner, and Gus quickly forced his way out the door in front of us without concern for his manners. He led us across the dirt driveway and the straw-covered ground and to the pavilion dining hall. Again, as soon as the door was opened, Gus rushed in. Steve saw us from across the dining hall and said, "I see you guys met Gus." Then he began to gently usher Gus back out the door, nudging him with his foot.

Gus was a Canadian goose. Months earlier, Steve's brother found two abandoned goose eggs and decided to incubate them. One egg hatched, and it was Gus. Birds identify with whatever life-form takes care of them upon arrival. As Gus pecked his way through the shell, there peering over the edge of the incubator were Steve and his family. As far as Gus was concerned, he was part of the new family and that is where he found his identity. He had no idea he was a goose.

Several days into the camp, after the middle school students became familiar with their surroundings, chasing Gus became an excellent outlet for entertainment. The first time I saw this, I was alerted by a desperate honking noise behind me. Turning that direction, five 12 and 13-year-old boys were antagonizing Gus by chasing and corralling him. Gus would run frantically with outstretched wings flapping fiercely in order to achieve maximum capacity goose-running speed. After cornering him, the students would back off, laughing hysterically, and leaving Gus dejected, defeated, and embarrassed.

That afternoon, I asked Steve why Gus put up with such antics. I wondered why he didn't spread those huge wings and take off flying above his enemies. Much to my amazement, I was informed that Gus did not fly. "You mean he is hurt and cannot fly?" I wondered. "No," Steve said. "You mean he doesn't know how to fly?" I asked. "Well, kind of," he said. "Well then, exactly what are you saying?" I queried again. "I mean, Gus not only doesn't know how to fly, he doesn't even know that he can fly," Steve stated. Gus was physically capable of soaring over his adversaries based on his God-given attributes, yet found himself completely beaten by his foes because of lack of knowledge. He was suffering with mistaken identity.

Gus would have been so much better off if he only knew he had the inherent ability to fly above his adversaries. As a result of our discussion, Steve decided to attempt to teach this adolescent goose more about his God-given identity. Change was not going to come easily for Gus. Although he wasn't living at full capacity in his life, he didn't know any better and had settled into mediocrity, accepting his plight. One afternoon when the students were in their small group sessions, Steve went out by the lake to find Gus. As was his custom, Gus immediately made himself at home right under Steve's feet. He reached down and gently picked Gus up in his arms. At a fast pace, due to Gus being quite irritated, Steve moved to the end of the dock where, without hesitation, he threw Gus as high as possible out over the lake. It wasn't a pretty sight. Clumsily flapping his wings, Gus came careening down to the water like a lame duck. As you would imagine, Gus was quite disgusted at the whole ordeal. He hastily paddled his way under the dock and to the shore. Gus didn't like the water either. Odd, huh! As he shook the water off his body, Steve quickly cornered him again. He picked him up with fully extended arms to avoid Gus' flailing efforts to snap at him, he once again carried Gus out on the dock and cast him out over the water. This time, much to my surprise, Gus flapped his wings several times, flew a few feet, and then gave up, crashing headfirst into the calm water. The process continued. On the fourth try, he flew 10 to 20 yards before executing a rough but safe landing. With Gus thoroughly perplexed, Steve ended the flying lesson for the day.

The next afternoon I was sitting at a picnic table near my cabin when I heard a familiar commotion ensue. As expected, the students were chasing Gus again. Gus immediately defaulted into his old techniques to avoid them at first. As usual, they were futile. God did not design a goose for sprinting. The students almost had Gus cornered near a large pine tree when he reversed direction tearing out through them, honking, and running full speed toward the water's edge. About twenty feet from the shore he began flapping his wings as God had created him to do. He slowly lifted off the ground right at the edge of the water and flew away from his adversaries some distance before landing near the water's edge of the lake. Gus had successfully made his first of many solo flights.

Gus was always physically capable of soaring over his adversaries based on his God-given attributes, yet found himself completely beaten by his foes because of lack of knowledge. In Christ the believer has been given everything necessary for life and godliness. He is redeemed to soar on wings like eagles! That is what this book is about… living in the full inheritance Christ has given you… for His glory!

Chapter 1

Ready to Jump!

On Memorial Day each year the swim club near my home would open the swimming pool for the summer. To celebrate the opening there would be an all-day party with games and food. The big event that day was always a game where buckets of coins were dumped into the pool for the children and teens to dive in and gather to keep. At the shallow end were pennies. As the pool grew deeper the coins grew more valuable. At the deep end of the pool there were silver dollars. In order to dive into the deep end of the pool you had to be a teenager as well as have enough experience to swim 15 feet down to collect the coins. Oh how I wished I was old enough and experienced enough to dive into the deep end of the pool. While I was dredging around for pennies, nickels and dimes, those in the deep end of the pool were pulling up dollars. They were experiencing a much richer reward.

It is my viewpoint that many Christians are fully aware that there is a spiritually deep end of the pool with great reward, but they find themselves trapped in the shallow end. They are experiencing far less than Biblically promised.

Christ desires a supernaturally empowered existence for His children. He says in John 10: 10b... *"I have come that they may have life, and have it to the full."* This fullness or abundance spoken of can be defined like this... knowing Christ intimately and experiencing a supernatural love, acceptance, power, and security found only in Him. This lifestyle is not only possible but promised. But let's be realistic. How many believers do you know that are living in supernatural abundance? Many are barely hanging in there? Their existence is little more than cyclically navigating the same old stuff; the same old chase; the same old empty results; the same old issues; the same old outcomes; the same old self. Do you find yourself living in this spin of despair? The results are paralyzing doubt and despair.

I want to introduce you to Will. He escaped the shallow end of the pool and began to experience the supernatural transformation found at the deep end of the pool! He had a great family and a strong business mind. One day he entered a meeting with several work associates with the intent to solve a business issue. He was prepared to listen well and be open-minded. However, not long into the meeting the opposite took place. Feeling that one associate was questioning his perspective, he reacted with high levels of control basically shutting down the discussion and creating a negative atmosphere that left everyone involved frustrated. The team walked away further apart and further away from a decision. His dictatorial control deflated any team morale.

Will experienced this controlling reaction frequently and it was not limited to the workplace. When he was questioned it always seemed like a personal attack to him. How could he escape this spin of despair?

Ginny escaped the shallow end of the pool and began to experience the supernatural transformation found at the deep end of the pool!

Ginny was a thirty-four-year-old wife and mother of two. After a minor disagreement with her husband she fell to the floor in a tearful fit. Her loving family stood helplessly in the wake of this painful outburst. Every two or three weeks she would cascade into emotional distress plunging into angry outbursts. She felt out of control and full of shame. It felt like others, particularly her family, were purposely provoking her. She hated these episodes but couldn't seem to do anything about them. How could she escape this spin of despair?

Cory escaped the shallow end of the pool and began to experience supernatural transformation found at the deep end of the pool!

Cory was happily married and the father of one son. As he returned from an out-of-town engagement he found himself consumed by lustful thoughts. He was returning from a Christian conference where he was the keynote speaker, and you would think that there would be nothing further from his mind. Dwelling on mental pornography he began to adventure in his mind toward the idea of stopping at a roadside strip bar not far down the road. This was not something that he had done before, but any sane reasoning was overwhelmed by intense feelings of excitement and consideration. He pulled into the parking lot of the strip bar. Nervously and with his heart about to beat out of his chest he made his way into the night spot. The initial thrill immediately dissipated into overwhelming guilt. He hurriedly left the strip bar, distressed and aware that he had gone over the edge.

From a young age Cory struggled with internet pornography. At 19 he came into a relationship with Christ and was sure that this habit would be the first to go. There was a temporary reprieve but when it returned it came on fast and furious. He managed his issues through the hope that came from temporary sobriety and justification. His wife was totally clueless of his struggle.

This experience with the strip bar scared Cory. He found himself entangled in the secret world of pornography and was crossing over the line into behavior that was devastating his life and family. On the way home he was ashamed and afraid. No amount of justification could quiet his concern. How could he escape this spin of despair?

This book is about how these people found victory. All of these stories have one thing in common. Each is real and all of them are sincere Christians. You may know them. You certainly know someone like them. Your story may be very similar to one of them. If not, one thing is for sure, you have your own story.

The other common denominators in each of these stories are pain and hope. For each there was a time, and sometimes a long time, where their situation seemed painful and hopeless. They stood helplessly in the shallow end of the pool wondering why they couldn't dive into the deep end. Things changed! Now they experience ever-increasing peace and victory. Their despair turned to brokenness, leading to a hope in Christ alone. God's promises are alive and the pathway to victory is clear. They each know Christ in a way that they never thought possible and experience His unconditional, indescribable love and blessings! Each of them identified and escaped the spin of despair and experienced supernatural transformation in their lives. They truly experienced "taking the gospel to heart." They were experiencing their new identity in Christ. The work of Christ on the cross promises this for His children.

Recently, following a sermon at our church, a man said to our pastor… "Hey, I get that I am a sinner, and I hear that I need to "trust Christ"… "trust the power of the Gospel," "take the gospel to heart." I just don't know how to do it on a daily basis" This man's comment is all too real. At least this gentleman had the guts to ask.

Without understanding how to apply the gospel daily and access its power on a moment-by-moment basis, the believer is left to his own methods to attempt to live for God. One result is moralistic effort that is a mere counterfeit that results in ultimate failure and misery. Another result is feeling that His promises are never quite accessible due to personal sin leading to guilt, shame, and despair. As a result many simply give up and accept spiritual mediocrity, which is really defeat. Ultimately the result is spiritual cynicism and hopelessness… whether communicated outwardly or not. What a sad state… sitting in the shallow end knowing that there is a deep end.

Does the name Dr. John S. Pemberton ring any bells? Maybe not, although his invention is a familiar household name making billions of dollars across the world. In 1866, this pharmacist by trade perfected what we know today as Coca-Cola. He died in 1869, only three years after his invention. He died a poor man without ever knowing the joy or financial benefits of his creation.

This story has a certain familiar ring to many Christians. After genuinely accepting Jesus Christ into their lives, many will go about their daily tasks without ever really knowing intimacy with Christ and enjoying the fruits of their relationship with Him.

Many believers are caught in the spin of despair and crying out to know how to apply the gospel to their daily lives. They starve for the Biblical promises of intimacy, identity, and influence… for the freedom, peace, and true satisfaction only found in Christ. That was their hope when they initially accepted Christ. The human heart cry, while sometimes not clearly verbalized, can easily be heard. It can be seen through wild chases after worldly facades, mirages that will only evaporate right before our very eyes. It can be seen in the lives of believers who settle for far less than what God promises. This book is not about health and wealth but about the central truths in God's word and the supernatural blessings that are found in Christ alone. It is a book about how to genuinely experience the release of these promises. It is about how Will, Ginny, Cory and yes, you and me can experience the full riches of our great God.

This book is intended to help the believer overcome confusion and understand the power of the gospel and how it applies to their daily life. Hosea 4:6 says, "My people are destroyed from lack of knowledge." There is hope! There is even a guarantee of victory. The question is… How powerful is the good news? The work of Christ on the cross is powerful. He is truly our freedom fighter. That was his mission!

Luke 4: 18 – 21 describes His mission…

"The Spirit of the Lord is on me, because He has anointed me to preach good news to the poor. He has sent me to proclaim freedom for the prisoners and recovery of sight for the blind, to release the oppressed, to proclaim the year of the Lord's favor. Then He rolled up the scroll, gave it back to the attendant and sat down. The eyes of everyone in the synagogue were fastened on Him. "Today this scripture is fulfilled in your hearing."

Let's jump into the deep end of the pool!

 Think about it!

1) Which of the following do you most identify with: Will, Ginny, or Cory and why?

2) John 10: 10b says… "I have come that they may have life, and have it to the full." Do you believe most believers are experiencing Christ's abundance? Why or why not?

3) When you are trying to deal with a fleshly challenge and you hear someone say something like…"take the gospel to heart," what does that mean to you?

4) The author states that many believers are caught in the "spin of despair." What do you think he means?

5) For you, what does it mean when you are challenged to "jump into the deep end of the pool?"

Chapter 2

The Root of the Problem

Will, Ginny, and Cory jumped into the deep end of the pool and discovered spiritual victory in their daily lives. It's scary, but the outcome is great. The begging question is why are we so desperate? How did we get so broken? Why can't Will, Ginny, Cory, you, and me get a grip? It is impossible to fully understand the answers to these questions without completely grasping the creation story and the impact of original sin in every man's heart. Without it we cannot wholly grasp the spiritual battles we encounter, God's great redemptive work, and how to experience God's full measure of blessing in Christ. Being reminded of our "roots" is the vital backdrop for our journey to experience freedom in Christ.

This narrative of Genesis 1 – 3 is intended to provide insight into the desperation of the human race and how it affects both those without Christ as well as those who know Him. To discover true freedom in Christ one must understand where the journey began.

Narrative of Genesis 1 - 3

His Delight… All Adventure and No Fear

"It was good!" By God's standards, that means really good. Divinely created; right out of His unlimited imagination; spoken into existence. How is this possible? The human mind cannot comprehend, but those are the facts. And now He awaits His great finale before His much deserved rest. The best He saved until last. All of creation sits at this anticipatory threshold waiting for what the Creator Himself would categorize as "exceedingly good." Is it possible for God to do something so good that He Himself marvels? If so, the next day would be extraordinarily enthralling for Him.

As dawn seeped into the darkness overtaking the night, excitement filled the air. The heavenly splendor and the earthly home were quite ready to welcome their grand inhabitants.

The Creator took one last satisfying gaze at what was before turning His attention to what was to be. Now, with His gentle command, the ground stirred up its dust and it swirled into human shape. The Creator now breathed life into the nostrils of this lifeless being. There before God and all of creation stood man. A masterpiece of the creator perfectly suited and equipped for his noble existence, but not quite complete. The Creator said, "It is not good for man to be alone. I will make a helper suitable for him." Falling into a deep sleep at the Creator's touch with not even an inkling of awareness of need, a rib was removed from man giving God just what was needed to miraculously create woman. Had the Creator outdone Himself once again? Man certainly thought so! Flesh of my flesh… man and woman were ready to rule their domain. The Creator, bursting with love and delight, gazed at His beloved and unhindered, broke into dance over them. All was in order… created for God's glory and man's rich reward.

Man and Woman, uniquely created? Oh, yes, and how! In His image, unlike anything yet or ever again, enabling streams of sweet communion to flow between the Creator and created ones. Overwhelmed were the created ones with the delight the Creator demonstrated to them. Their insatiable appetite for intimacy and companionship found its gratifying pleasure in the Creator. It was just meant to be. Abounding rivers of love overflowed, yielding significance, honor, dignity, and creativity. Unhindered and richly blessed, who could have imagined anything more?

From Him life was derived and through Him it was sustained. Attached to Him, this incredible source of life and intimacy, man and woman could enjoy the plunder of their new existence. Chosen to be, chosen to procreate, chosen to do, and created with one purpose: to glorify their one true God. Their responsibility: abide in Him and steward that which the Creator created and fruitfully multiply. Resources were without limits. Created were they with prestige of position, power to rule, possessions to steward, and pleasures to enjoy; a king and queen, so to speak. Not because of what they had done, but because of who they were. They were God's beloved. Intimacy, Identity, and Influence was the overflow.

A Clear Warning

One vital precaution ruled the land. In their domain stood two trees: one, the tree of good and evil; the other, the tree of life. To partake of the tree of good and evil would open the created ones' minds to that which would only bring death and destruction. God's first and only rule was to stay clear of this travesty. Everything else was for the taking.

The Tragedy

Then tragedy struck. Satan was on the prowl. The created ones entertained the evil one, allowing him to play upon their heartstrings of passion. The evil one claimed deception on the part of the Creator. He said that the creator was holding back and "there was more; they were limited and could be like God." Could this lust for more be so intoxicating that, in the created ones' stupor, they would dare forget their Creator? The evil one had, and they would soon follow.

There in the garden, in one egotistical nightmare, the created ones obstinately disobeyed their Creator and contaminated all that was. Left tragically in the wake of their own demise were the created ones. Spiritually dead, destitute, disconnected, and empty, they found themselves in a kind of hell. The easy flow of intimacy that once existed with the Creator abruptly ceased, completely cut off.

The Results

Once intimately connected to the Creator and stewards of creation, the fallen "King and Queen" find themselves only a shell of their former selves. Emptiness and shame send them into hiding. They now neither possess the relationship with the Creator nor the overflowing blessings. They were meant to live, but find themselves fatal casualties of their fickle sinful disobedience. They are now spiritually dead and blind… lost, empty, and un-tethered from their maker. Their new reality sends them and those who would follow chasing down most any path for what might satisfy. All they possess is their own ego and their innate craving to experience the intimacy, identity, and influence they once had. Sadly, they don't even know they are lost.

Herein lays the motive for man's mad chase: they voraciously hunger to be what they were created to be. Now devoid, they hopelessly grope around in their dead and blind state chasing what they can to fill their innate cravings. Their only perceptible avenue, wholly deceiving as it is, is to try to fill their starvation for true intimacy, identity, and influence and turn to whatever might give a sense of fulfillment. To do this, each create their own system… they are now a sort of god. Their straw systems have their own set of values and rules in hopes of achieving true gratification. Yes, they are fickle, ever changing, and ultimately give no life, but this is their only hope. Empty as they are, these inept systems are man's only avenue to find the intimacy, identity, and influence he is famished for.

The typical targets for these fleshly chases are: passion, power, position, purpose, possessions, and pleasures. Since he no longer has intimacy with the creator, he seeks the created things. He makes them the object of his affection, his idols. These are now an end unto themselves. They are his gods.

This chase, of course, is only a mirage: illusions and delusions, mere facades, a counterfeit that only guarantees further emptiness. Yet man claws and fights for the mere crumbs of what he once had; and the world operates as the perfect playground for these insane chases. The evil one presents a never-ending array of potential distortions and perversions intending to lead man to his next dream, always ending in a short-lived and never-satisfying fix.

Summing it Up

All humans have the same desperate heart cry. In their blindness they don't even know it. Innately embedded in their complex nature is an emptiness that craves, but for what?

To understand a human, one must start at the root of the issue. In this way, they are all the same. They desperately chase.

Should one be shocked by foolish choices that some might make to fill this empty void? These choices really make fleshly sense. They explode out of a desperate attempt to attain what is missing. It is natural for someone to chase hard after what is missed. If one finds the chase too hazardous or simply empty, he is apt to sedate himself from his reality of loss. There is no excuse for this reckless behavior; it is simply understood. We are dead… separated from God!

Every person craves and desperately chases. Just watch and in only a few minutes this insidious effort is underway in the most benign situations among people…in the world, in the home, in the workplace; in the church; anywhere there are people. The battle ensues to determine who is on top; one's place in community, who the power brokers are, the qualifications to attain prestige, and how success is defined. It's a mean game. The rules are constantly changing, leaders are frequently toppled, communities are always fickle, and success is short-lived. The best one might hope for is to make it to the top only to face the reality that his climb will always end in ultimate futility and emptiness. Most, unable to "make it to the top," are left in the dust with a sense of greater emptiness and wondering what it might have been like to succeed.

This insane chase, the desperation and turmoil, are all about the loss, the cavern that separates man from the only source of true fulfillment. People are famished for communion with their Maker and the flood of intimacy, identity, and influence that is its overflow, but don't even know it. We need a miracle.

Understanding Idolatry…

When my children were very young an argument started in the back of our van between my six-year-old and three-year-old. After calling it down from the driver's seat with no results, I pulled the van over at a gas station. I opened the side door of the van to find out what all of the irritation was about. Unbelievably, my six-year-old son handed me a gum wrapper… I'm not kidding… trash. He had taken it from his younger sister and they were fighting for possession. For that moment, this piece of trash had become the object of their affection. It was their idol and they were fighting over it.

Ridiculous I know, but the flesh can take anything and make it an idol. Idolatry flourishes in many areas. In other words idolatry takes root anywhere a person can chase after meaning and gratification. Remember, before the fall of man, none of these things were evil. God made man to enjoy people, pleasure, and passion, to have position and possessions, and to experience power and influence. These were overflow that came with being a child of God. But now, after the fall, these have become the object of our affection… the very way we define ourselves as broken people.

The following chart gives areas where idolatry flourishes. Next to each one are examples. Please add several other examples to each area.

The Innate Craving… **Intimacy**

Indications that <u>people</u> are an idol?

Ex. Such as People Pleaser/ approval junkie/ vicariously living through others

Indications that <u>pleasure</u> is an idol?

Ex. Such as eating obsessions/ living from event to event/ too much time with hobby

Indications that <u>passion</u> is an idol?

Ex. Such as addictive behavior with pornography/ flirtatiousness

The Innate Craving… **Identity**

Indications that <u>position</u> is an idol?

Ex. Driven to achieve status/ willing to demean someone to achieve goal

Indications that <u>possessions</u> are an idol?

Ex. Must have certain quality of life to be happy/ never satisfied/ always need more

The Innate Craving… **Influence**

Indications that <u>power</u> is an idol?

Ex. Control freak/ jealous of others advancement/ need to be right

Indications that purpose is an idol?

Ex. Over-achiever/ out of balance lifestyle

The Answer!

Is there any possible answer? Is there a way for Almighty God, the Creator of the Universe to redeem His created ones and retain His divine character? Yes! It was one that not only protected His divine character but fully showcased it. No, he wasn't caught off guard, surprised, confused, desperate, or frustrated. We're talking the King of Kings… the Lord of Lords; the Holy One; the All Knowing One; the Almighty One; the Creator of the Universe. He had a plan and it would not be thwarted.

"For God so loved the world that He gave His one and only Son, that whoever believes in Him shall not perish but have eternal life. For God did not send His Son into the world to condemn the world, but to save the world through Him." John 3:16, 17

His name is Christ Jesus; His very son; one with Him; His very divine nature; God himself. No doubt painfully, but without reservation, Jehovah God sacrificed His only son to redeem His children…all of this driven from His character of divine love. It's a relational love story of sacrificial redemption. His children are the recipients. They are His beloved. He adores and dances over them.

The specific results of the mad chases will become crystal clear later in the book.

What does that mean to you?

For the one who hasn't yet accepted Christ: Does this make sense to you? Do you see that you, like all men, are a sinner and in need of forgiveness? Do you see that God sent His son to pay the penalty for your sin and die for you? Do you want to invite Christ into your life to rescue you, become your Lord, and restore you into a perfect relationship with almighty God? If so, our great God is miraculously raising you from spiritual death and giving you life… life eternal. You, this very moment, can begin a new journey with Christ… the relationship you're starving for. In Him you will discover your sustenance; the true bread of life; the intimacy, identity, and influence you innately hunger for.

To accept Christ may seem like a simple prayer, but it is a supernatural and miraculous life-giving step. He died so that you can live. May I invite you to accept Christ?

Simply but sincerely pray this prayer to God:

Father in heaven, I know that I am a sinner and as a result am separated from you. I know that you sent Christ to die for me so that I can live in communion with you. Today, I want to accept Christ into my life as my Savior and Lord. Make me what you want me to be.

If you prayed the prayer, praise God and congratulations! Now it's time for you to get fully engaged with how to walk daily with Christ.

For those of you who are already believers: Maybe you're on a great journey with Christ and you are hungering for more. Or maybe you hear the story of this abiding relationship with Christ and honestly, it just hasn't' been that way for you. Maybe you're tired and spiritually passive? Or maybe even feeling despair. The whole experience has been hollow.

Come with me. I've got great news for you. Christ is for real. He is chasing hard after you. Taste and see that Jesus Christ is the real deal.

How do most believers think the original sin of Adam and Eve impacts their everyday life?

Please list several results of this catastrophic event.

In Chapter 2 the author communicates that the world is the perfect playground for our fleshly chases, our idols. What do you think he means?

Please place a check by the answer that best describes your relationship with Christ
☐ **Have not yet accepted Christ**
☐ **Just accepted Christ**
☐ **Been a believer since** _____

As a result of original sin the author suggests that there are three unmet innate desires that all men crave. They are the desire for intimacy, identity and influence. How do people typically attempt to fill their craving?

Intimacy -

Identity -

Influence -

While we all chase hard to fill these voids through fleshly effort, which do you find

yourself mostly craving and what are symptoms that make you answer it that way? (Examples: people, power, position, purpose, possessions and pleasures)

How do you think your life would be different if you sensed you were closer to Christ and true intimacy, identity, and influence was fulfilled through that relationship?

Passage:

Let us fix our eyes on Jesus, the author and perfecter for our faith, who for the joy set before him endured the cross, scorning its shame, and sat down at the right hand of the throne of God.

Praise:

Worship Jesus. Thank him for loving you so sacrificially. Reflect on the depths of his sacrifice. Worship him as the author and finisher of your faith.

Ponder:

Ask God to show you those areas of your heart where people or things cause your gaze to be distracted.

Pray:

Jesus, my passion is for my eyes to be fixed on you. Grant me the grace and strength to quickly turn my heart back to you so that I can drink deeply of you, Living Water, who always satisfies.

Chapter 3

The Fleshly Spin of Despair

This book is about true gratification! Of course trusting Christ is the answer. But what does that really mean? Many believers have tried but it just isn't working too well. All of God's children are precious to him. There is no story too simple or complex. There is no one too far away from His redemptive hand. His attention is on you! How do we focus on Christ? How do we escape the worldly perspective, temptations, and habits we so often fall victim to? How do we find victory over our idols? How do we enjoy our new identity in Christ? Come join me as we jump into the deep end of the pool!

In this chapter I would like to begin introducing a pathway to victory that can help all believers understand their personal uniqueness and how to promote greater reliance upon Christ. It has helped me and many others unfold our personal journeys in a way that makes sense. My hope is that this simple pathway, empowered by the incredible promises of God's word, will help you fully engage with Christ, enjoy the overflow of blessings, and better relate with others. You will discover your thought patterns, their foundations, and how to bring them into captivity in Christ and experience His transformational power from the inside out.

As mentioned before, to move forward in this material, it will demand humility, authenticity, teach-ability, brokenness, and dependency... all of which fly in the face of our fleshly pride. The outcome for those who have persevered on this journey in the past is that they have a whole new understanding of God's love, power, and promises found in a revitalized walk with Christ.

To begin introducing you to this pathway to victory we will dig into Will's story. In the appendix we will revisit with Ginny and Cory to see how their life stories progressed.

Will's Story

Will and I had been friends for a long time. He was a good family man, very encouraging, fun to be with, very committed to his business, and serious about his walk with God. Many times I have seen God powerfully use him to love and encourage those in need.

One day the two of us met for lunch. When Will arrived I could see that he was sullen. After a few minutes he opened up and shared. He explained that he had just come from a meeting with two work associates in his company. He said they had concerns about several of his business decisions. He further shared he felt he was being treated like a business rookie and the discussion felt personally condescending. He explained he entered the discussion with a commitment to listen well, be open, and attempt to find agreement. But as things progressed he spiraled into a negative frame of mind. To him their perspective felt like a personal attack.

Meeting 1

(joining in conversation after initial greetings)

Matt: Well how have things been?

Will: *You'll have to forgive me. I'm just totally frustrated! They have no idea what is really going on. They might think they mean well, but they just don't get it.*

Matt: I am sorry. Do you want to talk about it or just leave it alone?

Will: *What is there to talk about? It seems pretty clear. I'll just have to get over it.*

Matt: No, really, why don't you tell me what happened.

Will: *Just another day at the office… a bad experience with a couple of co-workers. I was trying to get to the bottom of a problem and come to an agreeable solution and it all fell apart. Somehow, even with intentions to listen well and create "buy in" from my associates, it all fell apart.*

Matt: Do you mind sharing how it ended?

Will: *I basically shut down. I did stand my ground… but I mostly just shut down.*

Matt: How did you stand your ground?

Will: *I made it clear that it is what it is. I am the team leader. I am not changing anything.*

Matt: What was their reaction?

Will: *One of them sat quietly while the other was angry. She muttered something about me being closed minded and unwilling to listen. Now that really got my blood boiling.*

Matt: What did you do then?

Will: *I just shut down. I had nothing else to say. I am in charge anyway so my best option was just close the meeting. I am just angry! I don't know what good it will do to keep hashing it out. I've just got to get over it.*

Urgent Instructions:

We have introduced Will, Ginny, and Cory. We will focus on Will throughout the book.

It is now your turn. You will need a story from your life to apply the vital principles as they unfold throughout the book. The best way to determine "your story" is to identify a common experience where you tend to become reactive or protective. These experiences often arise from a sense of being threatened through circumstances or a person. Sometimes this is referred to as "pushing someone's buttons." Please take a few minutes to reflect on your personal tendencies as you fill out the following "Personal Reflections" as carefully as possible. Please be specific and honest. **Please do not skip this vital step!**

Personal Reflections 1

The Fleshly Spin of Despair - What's your Story?

Below, please share an experience in the recent past where you felt significant frustration. If possible, share an experience that creates a quick negative reaction... a touchy area...so to speak. The experience can be from within the family, at work, or elsewhere.

What happened?

Who was affected?

How did it make you feel?

How did it end up?

Identifying the Fleshly Spin of Despair

Will faced a challenge in the workplace that created a significant reaction. As a result of the encounter, he initially reacted by shutting down and taking control. The emotional aftermath within his heart was complex and painful. No doubt that was also true with his associates.

Observation:

Each individual has a fairly predictable fleshly pattern when facing challenge. It is vital for each believer to identify and understand their unique fleshly patterns to progress toward experiencing true freedom in Christ. I refer to this pattern as the **Fleshly Spin of Despair.** All people have their own version of the fleshly spin of despair and unfortunately some do not move beyond it. This is sometimes due to a lack of knowledge or blind spots, at other times a result of pride, and sometimes their issues simply feel too painful to face. The result of the fleshly spin destroys joy, growth, success, and relationships. The spin of despair is the believer's fleshly mindset. It is one's state of mind due to the impact of original sin and our fallen nature activated by individual life experiences. It is the "carnal" state. The believer is constantly tempted to trust this undesirable mindset. We will discuss this in detail in later chapters. For now, let's examine the fleshly spin of despair by looking into Will's experience.

Stage 1 - People Involved & Perceived Threat

The fleshly spin of despair is provoked when people sense a perceived fleshly threat in their life. In other words, something provokes them to move into a protective state to guard their pride… their perceived identity (self-image), influence (self-worth), or sense of intimacy (relational connections). The specific threat can take many forms, but the catalyst is often another person.

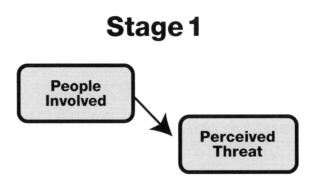

 Think about it!

In Will's case, who seemed to be the catalyst?

What seemed to be the perceived threat for Will?

Do you think that he was disappointed in the outcome of the meeting with his two associates? If so, why?

Personal Reflections 2

The Fleshly Spin of Despair - Stage 1

1. In your story, who served as the catalyst?

2. What was the perceived threat?

3. How did you handle it?

Stage 2 - Initial Feelings

Following the perceived threat, each person experiences an "initial feeling." The **initial feeling** often fits into one of three categories...**anger, fear, or hurt**... or some combination of the three. It is common for people to develop one of the three as their "go to" response when feeling threatened no matter what the provocation is. Have you ever known someone that seemed to always react to a perceived threat with the same initial feeling... either anger, hurt, or fear?

As you look at Will's story, which "initial feeling" did he have?

        Anger   Hurt   Fear

Observation:

If you said anger, I would agree. As you listen to the conversation, you can perceive other emotions as well. But he specifically said he was angry. It is difficult to move beyond the "initial feeling." Some find themselves stuck with their first impression becoming their permanent perspective. They find it almost impossible to move beyond this surface level. All of us have been told to count to ten before you react. This is to protect ourselves and others from a first impression that may prove to be destructive.

The following graph shows where we are on the pathway in Will's story. There were two co-workers involved. He felt threatened because he perceived they challenged his leadership and accused him of not listening. The result for Will was an initial feeling of anger.

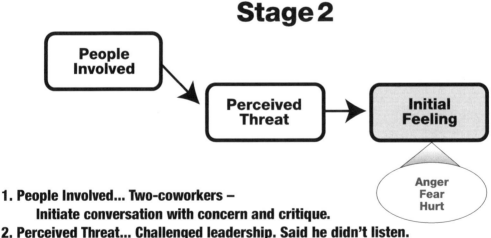

1. **People Involved... Two-coworkers –**
    Initiate conversation with concern and critique.
2. **Perceived Threat... Challenged leadership. Said he didn't listen.**
3. **Initial Feeling... Anger.**

Personal Reflections 3

The Fleshly Spin of Despair - Stage 2

1. Based upon your personal story, which "initial feeling" did you experience?

        Anger   Hurt   Fear

2. Would you say that when you face various threats in your life that your initial feeling tends to be the same?

3. If so, list a couple of other encounters where this was true.

    Some of you are excited about this journey. I can't wait to share with you the truths that have radically impacted my life and so many others. Some of you are rightfully skeptical. I've been there! The possibility of experiencing true communion with God that leads to a life of freedom and victory sounds incredible. But can it really be? It can! However, it isn't a road without challenge. As you can already see, it will demand slowing down and investing time and concentration throughout the study. It will demand humble, honest, and authentic self-appraisal that will expose flawed beliefs, attitudes, and actions. The journey doesn't always feel good. It may take unexpected twists and turns. But it always ends in greater intimacy with Christ and true blessing.

    The Gospel is complete. Through Christ we are secure for eternity in our new relationship with God. We are equally secure that our sanctification (spiritual growth) will continue and move us to greater maturity in Christ. But the work of sanctification is a work in progress in our lives. Spiritual growth is a journey. Of course we want instant fulfillment... no more pain, no more insecurity, no more wild chases... just happiness and delight. Only heaven will rescue us from this journey. While the journey on earth is difficult, it is good and purposeful! It provides God a stage to showcase His incredible love and faithfulness to believers as well as the world around them. God is committed to our sanctification. By way of sanctification our great God, through the power of the cross, sifts out our dependence upon the world and truly satisfies us with His intimate love, true identity, and eternal influence.

    In the next chapter we will continue our examination of the Fleshly Spin of Despair. You will find it eye-opening, possibly painful, and critical in the journey to Christ-centered freedom... Take the Gospel to Heart.

Passage:

Philippians 3:7-8

But whatever was to my profit I now consider loss for the sake of Christ. What is more, I consider everything a loss compared to the surpassing greatness of knowing Christ Jesus my Lord, for whose sake I have lost all things. I consider them rubbish that I may gain Christ.

Praise:

Exalt the surpassing greatness of Jesus Christ. He is King of kings, Lord of lords, Savior, Redeemer, and calls us his friend.

Ponder:

Ask God if there are areas in your life where your life where a "loss" would not be considered rubbish compared to knowing Christ. Also ask God to show you what your are holding on to more than him.

Pray:

God, it is easy to say that anything I could obtain or profit in this world pales in comparison to the love and life I find in you, but sometimes it is harder to live out that belief. Bring me into deeper and deeper intimacy with you, so that I might understand the surpassing greatness of knowing you.

Chapter 4

The Fleshly Spin of Despair
(Part 2)

et's continue our journey to discover our true identity in Christ. Last session we began looking at the Fleshly Spin of Despair. We considered the people involved, the perceived threat and the initial response. We will now look at Stage 3… Inward Reaction.

Stage 3 - Inward Reaction

When someone senses they are threatened, they not only experience an initial feeling, they also experience an inward reaction to that threat. Will's initial feeling was anger. The initial feeling is similar to the inward reaction in that it can present itself as a pattern of thinking… but not necessarily. Listed below are four common inward reactions:

Inward Reactions…

Blame - feeling that someone else is responsible for your pain
Shame - sensing dishonor, unworthiness, or embarrassment
Denial - treating circumstances as if they did not happen or are unimportant; to ignore or literally reconstruct facts
Sedate - attempting to deaden the pain through the overuse of chemicals, both prescription as well as other…alcohol, drugs, etc. Sedating could also include an overuse of otherwise healthy activity (work, recreation, exercise, sex) in order to produce natural chemical releases within the body or an emotional high. Note the graph on the following page.

 Think about it!

**As you look at Will's story, what was his inward reaction?
Why do you think this is so?**

Observation:

In Will's case blame was his initial inward reaction. As the discussion developed, there appeared to be a bit of denial when he said... "I am just angry! I don't know what good it will do to keep hashing it out. I've just got to get over it."

Let's look at the fleshly spin of despair in its third stage.

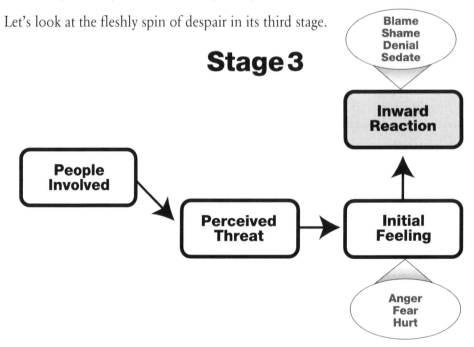

1. **People Involved... Two-coworkers –**
    Initiate conversation with concern and critique.
2. **Perceived Threat... Challenged leadership. Said he didn't listen.**
3. **Initial Feeling... Anger.**
4. **Inward Reaction... Blame.**

Personal Reflections 4

The Fleshly Spin of Despair - Stage 3

1. Based upon your personal story, put a check by the Inward Reaction that you felt.

Inward Reactions…

☐ **Blame** - feeling that someone else is responsible for your pain

☐ **Shame** - sensing dishonor, unworthiness, or embarrassment

☐ **Denial** - treating circumstances as if they did not happen or are unimportant. To ignore or literally reconstruct facts

☐ **Sedate** - attempting to deaden the pain through the overuse of chemicals, both prescription as well as other…alcohol, drug, etc.
Sedating could also include an overuse of otherwise healthy activity (work, recreation, exercise, sex) in order to produce natural chemical releases within the body or an emotional high.

2. Please be specific about how you inwardly reacted (thought process) to the particular perceived threat.

Stage 4 - Outward Disposition (Reaction)

The Outward Disposition is the way one displays their initial feeling towards others. Let's pick back up with Will and Matt in their conversation. Look for how Will expresses himself (outward disposition) to his co-workers.

Conversation Continues:

Matt: How do you think your co-workers perceived your actions?

Will: *What exactly do you mean by that? I don't really care.*

Matt: I know you better than that.

Will: *I guess it is what it is. They think that I am a jerk who isn't willing to listen to their input.*

Matt: So you would say unwilling to listen, maybe defensive. Any other thoughts about their perception?

Will: *Yeah, I certainly think they thought I was controlling and withdrew.*

How would you describe Will's outward disposition with his co-workers?

How do you think his co-workers would describe their experience when leaving the meeting?

Observation:

When someone feels threatened, their initial feeling (anger, fear, hurt) will always spawn an inward reaction (blame, shame, denial, sedate) which will manifest itself through their outward disposition. This outward disposition can be expressed openly or passively. The following are common passive responses:

obstructing

fostering chaos

procrastinating

creating emotional walls in relationships

This disposition can be expressed both initially as well as long term.

As I talked with Will he seemed in touch with his outward disposition and how his co-workers perceived him. Sometimes people are able to see themselves through the eyes of others and sometimes they cannot. It is important for a person to have a realistic picture of how their outward disposition (behavior) is perceived and how it impacts others in order to both realistically understand the event as well as to know how to later restore the relationship if called for.

The following are other examples of potential outward dispositions...

Unapproachable	**Non-teachable**
Unwilling to listen	**Jealousy**
Resentment	**Unwise behavior**
Withdrawal	**Unwilling to take risk**
Weak/ Pleaser	**Protective**
Controlling	**Strong willed**
Defensive	**Sarcastic humor**
Judgmental	**Independent**
Overly sensitive	**Insensitive**
Prideful	**Closed minded**

Which of the passive or aggressive reactions do you typically respond? Circle any that apply in the previous description.

Note that "outward disposition" has been added to the graph with the arrow pointing to the people who are impacted.

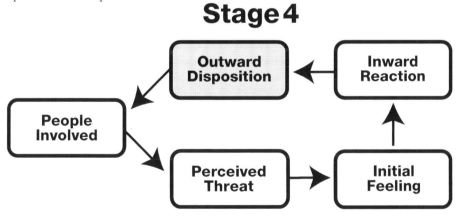

1. People Involved... Two-coworkers – Initiate conversation with concern and critique.
2. Perceived Threat... Challenged leadership. Said he didn't listen.
3. Initial Feeling... Anger.
4. Inward Reaction... Blame and later shame
5. Outward Disposition... Controlling/ Withdrew/ Wouldn't listen

Early in this study I invited you to participate by sharing a personal life story within the Personal Reflections. Often, at this point, participants realize that they have a better example than the one originally selected that exemplifies the spin of despair. Please feel free on Personal Reflection 5 to continue with the same life example or change to a new one now that you understand more of the process.

Personal Reflections 5

The Fleshly Spin of Despair - Stage 4

Based upon the person story you shared from the recent past please answer the following questions.

Review:
In your story, who served as the catalyst?

What was the perceived threat?

1. My initial feeling was...

    Anger   Hurt   Fear

2. My inward reaction was...

    Blame   Shame   Denial   Medicate

3. My outward disposition was...

Unapproachable	Non-teachable	Unwilling to listen
Jealousy	Resentment	Unwise behavior
Withdrawal	Unwilling to take risk	Weak/Pleaser
Protective	Controlling	Strong willed
Defensive	Sarcastic	Judgmental
Independent	Overly sensitive	Insensitive
Prideful	Close minded	Obstructing
Fostering chaos	Creating emotional walls	Procrastinating

4. How do you think your outward disposition affected others and your relationship with them?

Summing up the Fleshly Spin of Despair

When talking to Will you can see that his initial impression was his momentary reality. In other words, his feelings were currently serving as his reality. Immediately following a perceived threat it is natural for people to embark on the fleshly spin of despair. Unfortunately, some find themselves held captive to this mindset.

The great news is that in Christ's power believers can identify this fleshly response and deal with the spin of despair. They can know the freedom that comes by quickly identifying these fleshly tendencies and move quickly to Christ-centered truth. If they don't know how to do this, they may become trapped in The Fleshly Spin of Despair with all of its unpleasant results.

If not dealt with the person typically builds a stronger case and becomes more convinced of their fleshly perspective. These cycles may go for long periods of time (even permanently), and their feelings may remain their reality with their disposition exhibiting it. Understanding it and knowing how to escape it is vital. Some believers live in constant defeat as a result of being captive in the fleshly spin of despair. They are detached from Biblical truth that promises to lead to freedom. Unfortunately, no one completely escapes the spin of despair. Every believer will find themselves fighting the flesh and the spin of despair. The question is how quickly they can identify it and seek Christ for freedom.

Each believer's fleshly pattern produces particularly vulnerable areas where they are more apt to get stuck in the fleshly spin of despair. These cycles are emotionally unhealthy as well as relationally debilitating. Have you ever met someone who always seems angry, hurt, or fearful? It is quite easy to spin in the reactive cycle of the fleshly spin of despair. Within this unhealthy superficial spin the individual usually only seeks validation for their "reality" and their levels of blame, shame, denial or sedating are raised to meet the ever increasing pain. Below is a picture of the Fleshly Spin of Despair.

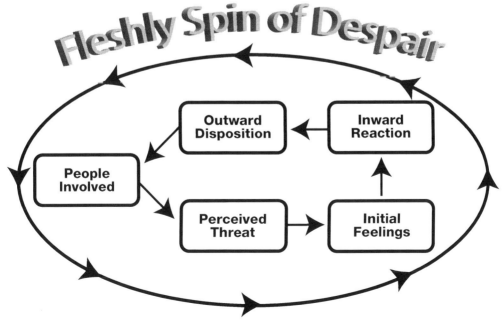

Personal Reflections 6

The Fleshly Spin of Despair - On a Broader Basis

Thinking on a little broader basis, what typically creates the greatest sense of fleshly threat?

I feel threatened when…

1. What is your typical initial feeling?

      Anger   Hurt   Fear

Please describe in greater detail.

2. What is your typical inward emotion?

      Blame Shame   Denial   Medicate

Please describe in greater detail.

3. What is your typical outward disposition?

Unapproachable	Non-teachable	Unwilling to listen
Jealousy	Resentment	Unwise behavior
Withdrawal	Unwilling to take risk	Weak/Pleaser
Protective	Controlling	Strong willed
Defensive	Sarcastic	Judgmental
Independent	Overly sensitive	Insensitive
Prideful	Close minded	Obstructing
Fostering chaos	Creating emotional walls	Procrastinating

Please describe in greater detail.

4. How do you think your outward disposition typically affects your relationships with others?

5. How far back can you remember this spin going on in your life?

As a result of the study you should now be able to identify and understand a personal example of the fleshly spin of despair from your own life. It is also quite possible that you see that this example and your response is not just an isolated reaction but a fleshly pattern. Either way, understanding this is a vital step to move toward incredible freedom in Christ. The believer is challenged by these fleshly reactions and patterns which are in place to protect sinful pride. Before we move to the next stage to further identify our specific tendencies and their origin, let's pause a moment to pray.

Passage:

1 Peter 1:3

Praise be to the God and Father of our Lord Jesus Christ! In His great mercy He has given us new birth into a living hope through the resurrection of Jesus Christ from the dead...

Praise:

Praise be to the God and Father of our Lord Jesus Christ! Revel in his glory, majesty, and power!

Ponder:

What does it mean to have a new birth into a living hope? How does God want this living hope to infuse your life today?

Pray:

God of mercy. What a beautiful name! Thank you that my living hope comes from the power of the resurrection. There is no struggle that is bigger than the power of the resurrection of Jesus Christ. Thank you for your mercy that allows me to come back to a new birth in a living hope as often as needed.

Chapter 5

Fleshly Foundational Beliefs

We have defined the fleshly spin of despair and attempted to apply it to your life story. You might be saying… "I understand the spin of despair a lot better." So what do I do with that information? Is self-knowledge helpful without hope for change? Am I stuck? Am I supposed to be depressed or embarrassed? We are almost down to the foundation, but not quite there. This next step will help you identify beliefs that serve as the foundation for the spin of despair so that we can properly deal with them.

All people naturally create Fleshly Foundational Beliefs (fleshly values) to measure their sense of self-worth. These measurements are our idols that are put in place, usually unconsciously, to determine one's value. As stated in chapter 2, these idols fill the void of intimacy, identity, or influence found only in a relationship with God which was lost at the fall. Idols can take many forms including people, pleasure, passion, position, possessions, power, and purpose. Look below at several fleshly foundational beliefs (idol) statements…

- I am successful when I achieve a high standard of living.
- I am significant when I am better than anyone else at what I do.
- I am accepted when everyone is pleased with me.
- I am content when things go as I planned.
- I am loved when…
- I am complete when…
- I am fulfilled when…

While these beliefs have a massive influence on our lives, typically we are not aware of them. These beliefs are the foundational impetus for the Fleshly Spin of Despair.

Where do these beliefs come from and what are the results?

To best understand their origin, let's take a theological dive into the deep end of the pool for a minute. Fleshly foundational beliefs are the bedrock of our manmade straw systems intended to bring life. But the opposite is true. This entrenched fleshly value system consistently serves as a stronghold, controlling the non-believer and wreaking havoc in the life of the believer. They are the result of the fallen nature (flesh) and its desire to promote and protect fleshly pride. Think back with me to the second chapter on the fall of man. We are born disconnected from God. At birth, born into sin, we are starving for what we were created to be. Without connection to the creator, who is the only true source of true identity and value, we find ourselves empty of true intimacy, identity, and influence. Each person creates their own straw system of belief (idols) to fill this void to prove they are lovable, unique, and purposeful.

These sets of beliefs serve as a base to process and determine our value or self-image (pride). It serves as the "standard" in hopes of experiencing self-love, self-identity, and self-worth. Of course these "things" never could and never will deliver the intended outcome. The real result is further emptiness emitting egotistical pride, insecurity, and insignificance. But man strives to say "it ain't so." All men have a carefully woven straw system that they are desperately chasing. Amazing! And we don't even know it. Furthermore, we go about protecting our image by attempting to convince others that we measure up. I have heard respected friends refer to this fleshly posturing as one's "false self" or the act of "posing." These are good descriptions. In other words, doing everything possible to prove to others we have value. All build their idol network of Fleshly Foundational Beliefs. If someone happens to step on our image, watch out. It ignites a fleshly spin of despair creating havoc within and often with others.

In this next gathering, Will discovers his Fleshly Foundational Beliefs...

Meeting 2: One week later Matt and Will meet at Matt's office

Matt: How have you been feeling since last week?

Will: *It's been a hard week. Still muddling through the experience I had with my associates.*

Matt: I know that this is beginning to sound like psycho-babble and I am certainly not a therapist, but let me ask you... What were your feelings on a deeper level when you were going through the experience with your associates?

Will: *I felt angry. Hurt.*

Matt: That is true. But were they hitting you on a deeper level? Deeper emotions than anger and hurt? What did you feel they were personally saying or insinuating about you?

Will: *Maybe like they really don't know me... like they were falsely judging me. They came in with a know-it-all attitude!*

Matt: When you say they really don't know you and were judging you, do you mean you felt misunderstood and disrespected?

Will: *They definitely misunderstood me and I definitely did not feel respected.*

Matt: Looking back, other than feeling misunderstood and disrespected, were their other feelings?

Will: *They were questioning my competence. You know, I've been doing that job a long time and have put my heart and soul into it. They have no idea. I hate it when that happens. Incompetence is not an option. The thought of them questioning me like that!*

Matt: I am sorry about what you've been through. I know you well and you are certainly not incompetent in the workplace. Do you think that they were intending to question your competence?

Will: *I don't know, but they did.*

Matt: Competency is obviously a high value for you. It plays directly into how you view yourself. Have you been hurt before by people challenging your competency?

Will: *It is a high value and I am sensitive to the issue. The truth is it always looms over me. I am constantly under pressure to prove myself. While most of the time I exist alright with it. I know that it affects all of my relationships. My typical response has just been to accept it as "the way I am" and move ahead. Anything less would be failure. There is no room for failure.*

Matt: Are you saying that to convince me or yourself?

Will: *That is how I have lived… but I am really tired and defeated. Even my Christian walk reflects this. I have been seeking harder than ever to grow in my faith but it seems the harder I try the further away I feel. Now I am just unloading on you. I'm sorry!*

Matt: No, please go ahead. I think you're getting to some important stuff. Finish this sentence for me based on what you're saying:

I must be completely competent in order to….

Will: *I must be fully competent in order to be successful. I'll add something to it… I must be fully competent, and have others see me that way, to be successful and valued.*

Matt: How is that playing out for you?

Will: *It is an impossible standard to reach. I could never reach my standard to be fully competent, and even if I could, not everyone would necessarily see it my way. Everyone has different standards. In the business world and in life in general, there needs to be openness and willingness for people to question situations and even sometimes disagree. My perspective certainly doesn't leave room for that.*

Matt: According to what you said, this view of success is something you have struggled with a long time? That is… finding your value through being competent.

Will: *It is definitely something that has been a challenge. I have always cared too much about how others view me and the need to prove myself. But interestingly, I am my worst critic. What do I do to snap out of this?*

Matt: Over the years we naturally develop self-imposed standards to prove our value. I call them Fleshly Foundational Beliefs. Let me specifically define what I am talking about… A fleshly foundational belief is a value (measurement) invoked by a person on themselves in order to prove and protect their sense of self-worth, or you could say, their pride. These standards can affect people their whole lives. Fill in these blanks for me…

I feel I am _____ when _____.

Will: *I feel I am successful and respected when I am fully competent at all times. What makes that worse is it is based upon perfectionist standards and in the eyes of others.*

Matt: Well done! That is a Fleshly Foundational Belief. You added a few caveat's on the end of the definition to further clarify. Can you imagine what "Will" would be like if he wasn't driven by the fear of incompetence and the pain associated with it? What would it be like to relax and know peace; not to wake up every day feeling the pressure to perform at a level that no one could accomplish; to accept situations even if they don't turn out right when you have done a reasonable job; to be able to accept critique that is not directed at you without personalizing it; to accept personal critique without defensiveness; to have relationships that are not competitive and friendships without stuffing issues.

Will: (with tears welling up in his eyes) *I cannot imagine an existence like you described. What do I do?*

Matt: I've got a graph for us to look at.

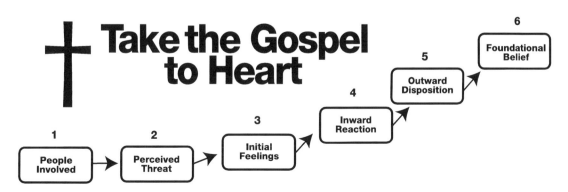

	1)	People Involved………..Two co-workers– initiate conversation with concern and critique
	2)	Perceived Threat………..Challenged leadership/ Said I didn't listen
	3)	Initial Feeling…………..Anger
	4)	Inward Reaction……….Blame and later shame
	5)	Outward Disposition….Controlling/ withdrew/ wouldn't listen
	6)	Fleshly Foundational Belief… I feel I am successful and respected when I am fully competent at all times. Another way of saying it is… To get approval I must be fully competent at all times based upon perfectionist standards not only in my eyes but in others' perspective.

Matt (Continues): See how we are breaking the fleshly spin of despair and now moving forward! This is because we are identifying the foundational beliefs that serve as the foundation for the fleshly spin of despair.

Will: *It makes a lot of sense. I even feel better knowing what is going on.*

Matt: Will, there is a certain catharsis that takes place in most people when they finally identify and understand their battle. But the real good news comes a bit later when you find victory through the cross. You're not unique. All believers have developed fleshly foundational beliefs. As I said earlier these beliefs originate out of our sinful flesh in an effort to build up and support our fleshly pride. They are a result of our fallen nature.

Will: *Do people typically have one major issue like this?*

Matt: The flesh is deceitfully wicked and we are full of challenges. But don't let that get you down. The work of Christ is plenty able to bring victory in every area. We'll take them one at a time. Let's keep focused on this one.

Will: *I will admit that I am pretty disappointed in myself. I thought that I was stronger than this. I thought that I had my spiritual life in better order. I misunderstood how powerful my flesh is and the battle it creates in me.*

Matt: The flesh is powerful. It does create great turmoil. Many get confused and are surprised when they face spiritual battles. I have an assignment that I would like for you to read before we meet again that might give you further insight on the flesh. Then we can talk about it when we meet. Next time we are together we will also look into other factors that inflame fleshly foundational belief.

Will: *Super! See you next week.*

Please answer the following questions…

What are Fleshly Foundational Beliefs?

Why do we have them?

Instructions: This is Will's Fleshly Foundational Beliefs worksheet. Please carefully look it over and then fill out the worksheet on the next page based on your life story.

Identifying Foundational Beliefs Worksheet

Definition: Foundational Beliefs are fleshly (values) standards invoked by someone on themselves by which they measure their self-worth. To identify potential foundational beliefs, please answer the following questions.

1. My "initial feeling" was...

    <u>Anger</u>   Fear   Hurt

2. My "inward reaction" was...

    <u>Blame</u>   Shame   Denial   Medicate

3. The experience made me feel... (circle any that apply)

<u>Misunderstood</u>	Incompetent	Unsafe	Unloved	Used
<u>Disrespected</u>	Unfairly treated	Not accepted	Belittled	Accused
Ridiculed	<u>Unsuccessful</u>	Insignificant	<u>Shamed</u>	Blamed
Insecure	Devalued	Loss of control	Talked down to	Immature
Unappreciated	Unheard	Afraid	Ignored	Left out
<u>Embarrassed</u>	Foolish	Condescended to	Unworthy	Unhappy
Condemned	Unworthy	Stupid	Unpopular	<u>Reputation threatened</u>
Worthless	Abused			

4. What did you feel the experience was saying or insinuating about you personally?
(Maybe the same answer you circled in question #3)

The experience made me feel I *am incompetent and a failure.*
(ex. I have little value/ I am a failure/ I am unlovable/ I am incompetent/ I don't deserve respect/ I am insignificant)

5. One of the identifiable characteristics of foundational belief is consistency. Have you experienced the feelings communicated in answer #4 before?

■ Yes ☐ No   How Often?   ☐ Seldom ☐ Regular ■ Frequently

6. What was the desired value you felt denied you in question #4?
(Discovered usually by considering the opposite of answer for question 4)

Desired Value: *Feel Valued and Successful*
(ex. Valued/ Successful/ Loved/ Competent/ Respected/ In Control/ Significant)

7. Based on the answer #6 (Desired Value), please fill in the blanks.

I must be	*fully competent know others see me as fully competent*	in order to	*feel valued and successful*
			(Desired Value)
When	*people doubt me, question me or don't do it my way*	it especially makes me feel	*incompetent and like a faliure*
			(Answer from #4)

Foundational Belief...

I feel I am <u>*successful and respected*</u> when <u>*I am fully competent at all times*</u>.
           (Desired Value)

Sample Answers:

	I am right	I am in charge	The plan is fail-safe	Things go perfectly
	I am admired	No negative feedback	Things stay the same	I am in the inner circle
No one talks about me	I am the best	People are pleased	I get the attention	I am not questioned
Know everything going on	I am in control	There is peace	Fully competent	I get the credit

Personal Reflections 7

Identifying Foundational Beliefs Worksheet

Definition: Foundational Beliefs are fleshly (values) standards invoked by someone on themselves by which they measure their self-worth. To identify potential foundational beliefs, please answer the following questions.

1. My "initial feeling" was...

                    Anger   Fear   Hurt

2. My "inward reaction" was...

                Blame   Shame   Denial   Medicate

3. The experience made me feel... (circle any that apply)

Misunderstood	Incompetent	Unsafe	Unloved	Used
Disrespected	Unfairly treated	Not accepted	Belittled	Accused
Ridiculed	Unsuccessful	Insignificant	Shamed	Blamed
Insecure	Devalued	Loss of control	Talked down to	Immature
Unappreciated	Unheard	Afraid	Ignored	Left out
Embarrassed	Foolish	Condescended to	Unworthy	Unhappy
Condemned	Unworthy	Stupid	Unpopular	Reputation threatened
Worthless	Abused			

4. What did you feel the experience was saying or insinuating about you personally?
(Maybe the same answer you circled in question #3)

The experience made me feel I
(ex. I have little value/ I am a failure/ I am unlovable/ I am incompetent/ I don't deserve respect/ I am insignificant)

5. One of the identifiable characteristics of foundational belief is consistency. Have you experienced the feelings communicated in answer #4 before?

    ☐ Yes ☐ No   How Often?   ☐ Seldom ☐ Regular ☐ Frequently

6. What was the desired value you felt denied you in question #4?
(Discovered usually by considering the opposite of answer for question 4)

Desired Value:
(ex. Valued/ Successful/ Loved/ Competent/ Respected/ In Control/ Significant)

7. Based on the answer #6 (Desired Value), please fill in the blanks.

I must be [_____] **in order to** [_____]
                                                         (Desired Value)

When [_____] **it especially makes me feel** [_____]
                                                         (Answer from #4)

Foundational Belief...

I feel I am _____ when _____.
                      (Desired Value)

Sample Answers:

	I am right	I am in charge	The plan is fail-safe	Things go perfectly
	I am admired	No negative feedback	Things stay the same	I am in the inner circle
No one talks about me	I am the best	People are pleased	I get the attention	I am not questioned
Know everything going on	I am in control	There is peace	Fully competent	I get the credit

Prayer Moments

Passage:

2 Peter 1:3-4

His divine power has given us everything we need for life and godliness through our knowledge of Him who called us by His own glory and goodness. Through these He has given us His very great and precious promises, so that through them you may participate in the divine nature and escape the corruption in the world caused by evil desires.

Praise:

Thank you, Father, for your divine power that gives me everything I need for life and godliness!

Ponder:

Each of us has time in our lives when we feel inadequate or incapable. What are some of those areas in your life? Ask God to show you how he has already provided everything you need for those areas.

Pray:

Lord, I want to know you and the knowledge of you that calls me to your own glory and goodness. Mold me into more of the reflection of your glory. Thank you that my victory is secure in you.

Chapter 6

The Flesh... a Formidable Foe!

The **ultimate direction of this book** is to discover the pathway to victory promised to every believer. We have looked at the fleshly spin of despair that challenges every believer. We have examined the fleshly straw system and their foundational beliefs that serve as the root for this fleshly despair. Ultimately, we are aimed at fully understanding the heart of the Gospel and its impact on our everyday life...how to take the Gospel to Heart! My desire is to see the power of our great God truly ignite within every believer in a way that transforms their heart from the inside out. To move to the next step, it is vital to understand why our flesh and the straw systems we create with our foundational beliefs can be such bullies.

Let's start with the ultimate hope we have in Christ. I can take comfort in Him knowing that nothing can interrupt my relationship with God. I have great relief that I am set free from the bondage and obligation to sin. But why do I keep sinning? God has done His part; how do I do mine? What is this massive undertow that pulls me toward sin?" Why do so many Christians seem to be losing the battle?

This daily battle is with our "flesh." As discussed earlier, before salvation, our nature was evil. When we accepted Christ, the old nature ("old self," Romans 6:6) that once held us hostage was crucified (rendered powerless) and no longer has control over us as it once did. However, within the believer there exists fleshly desire. It is our own desire to control and provide our own worldly means of satisfaction. We are no longer obligated to our flesh ("old man"), but one should not underestimate its potential to seek and act in control. As mentioned in an earlier chapter, the world is the perfect playground to allure and entertain the non-Christian. This is equally true for the flesh. This battle against temptation will be a constant one in our life (I John 1: 8-10). This is because our flesh remains in a corruptible state (apt to sin).

The flesh (old self) and its created system are busy and powerful, wreaking havoc in the believer every day. It is a bully. It is our old life before Christ trying to take back control. It obnoxiously rages within the believer trying to dominate. Our flesh does only what it knows to do... pridefully want to take control for position, power, and prestige and chase after temporary pleasure (lust of the flesh, lust of the eyes, pride of life). Through Christ, we are no longer our own, but God's. There is a new power broker in town...the true King; the Lord of Lords; the deliverer; the lover of our soul; the author and perfecter; the one who offers the way, the truth, and the life. It is a good thing that He is; and He will win out!

Our flesh resists God's control and attempts to bully us into selfish ambition and self gratification. It fights tooth and nail to control and seek glory. The Westminster Confession and Martin Luther speak about this issue.

Westminster Confession of Faith... Chapter IX - Section 4

IV. When God converts a sinner, and translates him into the state of grace, He frees him from his natural bondage under sin;[8] and, by His grace alone, enables him freely to will and to do that which is spiritually good;[9] yet so, as that by reason of his remaining corruption, he does not perfectly, or only, will that which is good, but does also will that which is evil.[10]

MARTIN LUTHER'S PREFACE TO THE GALATIANS
(Abridgment and paraphrase by T. Keller)

Now both these things continue while we live here. We are accused, exercised with temptations, oppressed with heaviness and sorrow, and bruised by the law with its demands of active righteousness. These attacks fall upon our "flesh" [--the part of our heart that still seeks to earn our salvation] ... Because of this, Paul sets out in this letter of Galatians to teach us, to comfort us, and to keep us constantly aware of this Christian righteousness. For if the truth of being *justified by Christ alone* (not by our works) is lost, then all Christian truths are lost. For there is no middle ground between Christian righteousness and works-righteousness; if you do not build your confidence on the work of Christ you must build your confidence on your own work. On this truth and only on this truth the church is built and has its being . . .

Many are seemingly shocked by the depravity of the flesh. Somehow Christians are lured into thinking that the process of sanctification involves the flesh growing more like Christ... that somehow it is being tamed and getting better with time. God's word teaches the opposite. The flesh continues to grow more corrupt with time in the believer.

Ephesians 4: 22

"You were taught, with regard to your former way of life, to put off your old self, which is being corrupted by its deceitful desires;"

Note in this passage, when referring to the old self, that it continues to become more corrupted with time. "Which is being corrupted" is spoken in the present perfect tense indicating its continual depravation. Let me remind you, in Christ we are no longer in bondage or obligated to this old nature, but it is still powerful and even more corrupted as each day passes.

I often hear stories of Christians who have miserably fallen to grievous sin. When they are in the public eye they often receive scathing judgment… both from the world as well as other believers. On one hand, I am hopeful for a different outcome, but on the other, we must understand the capability of the flesh. This is in no way to make excuse for sin; it is only to provide a sober look at the truth about man and about the capabilities of the believer controlled by his flesh and not by God's Spirit. Today, except for the grace of God, you and I can fall harder and further than we ever could before.

One thing is crystal clear. Nothing good comes from the flesh. Not before we were saved when it dominated our lives as a slave master or now, in its current weaker, but plenty irritating state. It is incapable of producing anything of eternal value. Our flesh will try to do anything to access control and build itself up. I cannot begin to count the times that I catch myself competing for position or power or using my gifts and talents for my own glory. I can twist anything to make it about me. Just as misleading, we often attempt to galvanize the best we have of our flesh with all the will power we can muster to try to live for God in our own strength. This robs the gospel of its power. It always ends in frustration and defeat. Even when used with good intention in mind, if we depend upon the flesh, it delivers impotently.

Like all aspects of spiritual growth, daily victory is only possible with Christ's empowerment and strength. But we often test our own effort before relying completely on Him. This is true in our initial step toward salvation (which must be reliant upon Christ alone). It is true for all aspects of sanctification (which must be reliant upon Christ alone). Utter dependence upon Christ alone is the only means to live a daily life of victory for God's glory.

When our children were young, we received two gerbils as a gift (one must appreciate friends like that). Although the little critters were free, we had to invest a small fortune into their housing, food, and of course, their exercise wheel. Every gerbil must have an exercise wheel! It is quite entertaining to watch the little rodents work out. They approach the wheel with confidence. Upon entering, they begin jogging at a medium pace. Before long, they are running so fast that the wheel takes control and the little fellows are flipped into oblivion. They roll out of the wheel dizzy and defeated, lap up some water, eat a little snack, take a little nap, and then return to the wheel again and again and again.

Unfortunately, the gerbil story hits too close to home for me, and I am sure, for many Christians. When faced with spiritual challenge, most believers climb onto a familiar wheel of self-effort and give it a hardy run in hopes of achieving spiritual victory. The results are always the same, spiritual defeat. With the best intentions, we fall prey to riding the fleshly "spin of despair." It is not long before the wheel has taken control, and we find ourselves dizzy and defeated. Some will ride the wheel for just a short time and simply give up, accepting that defeat is the Christian norm. Others, in the name of commitment, will embark on the wheel for years, believing some new discipline may be the secret that will manifest true spiritual fruit. However, the results are always the same. Either the result is a cheap imitation of true spiritual fruit or there is simply no fruit at all. If you have given the wheel your best try and given up or find yourself exhausted from continually running on the wheel of despair, I've got great news for you!

- God declares that we have inherited the fullness of Christ (Colossians 2:9-10).

- He has given us everything we need for life and godliness (II Peter 1:3-4).

- He promises that there is no temptation that we cannot escape (I Corinthians 10:13).

- He promises an abundant life (John 10:10).

- He promises the same incomparably great power that He exerted when He raised Christ from the dead (Ephesians 1:19).

- He says that "all the promises are yes for us in Christ Jesus." (II Corinthians 1: 20)

The promises are clear… and the empowerment is in place for the believer to pursue a Christ-centered life. He does not need to spin hopelessly on the wheel of despair or give up. The difference now is we have a new identity. We are no longer prisoners. We are not obligated to the flesh and its loud and demanding requests. But, you say, it sure feels powerful! It sure seems that the cell door has been re-sealed over me. You, my friend, are no longer a slave, but a son… a son of the most high… a son of the living God… an heir and co-heir with Christ. Come out. Our great God's work of salvation is complete and competent and he will set you free!

Think about it!

1. List several important points from "The Flesh… a Formidable Foe."

2. How do you think most believers view the flesh and its power?

3. What was the author's reasoning for sharing Ephesians 4: 22?

"You were taught, with regard to your former way of life, to put off your old self, which is being corrupted by its deceitful desires;"

How does that information affect your perspective of sin?

Do you have any specific applications?

4. What are areas where you felt/feel like the gerbils and their wheel?

Are you more apt to just give up when spun out of the fleshly wheel or re-embark with greater determination? Please explain.

5. How do these passages of hope affect you? (Circle one.)

    Excited   **Cautiously Hopeful**   **Pretty Skeptical**

- God declares that we have inherited the fullness of Christ (Colossians 2:9-10).
- He has given us everything we need for life and godliness (II Peter 1:3-4).
- He promises that there is no temptation that we cannot escape (I Corinthians 10:13).
- He promises an abundant life (John 10:10).
- He promises the same incomparably great power that He exerted when He raised Christ from the dead (Ephesians 1:19).
- He says that "all the promises are yes for us in Christ Jesus." (II Corinthians 1: 20)

Passage:

1 Thessalonians 5:23-24

May God himself, the God of peace, sanctify you through and through. May your whole spirit, soul and body be kept blameless at the coming of our Lord Jesus Christ. The one who calls you is faithful, and He will do it.

Praise:

Thank God for his faithfulness to you and his power to complete what he has begun. Worship God as your God of peace.

Ponder:

Ask God what it looks like for you to be made whole spirit, soul, and body.

Pray:

Father, our standard is perfection and wholeness, and you are not satisfied with less. Thank you that you don't leave it up to us to work harder or do more to meet that standard. You are faithful to sanctify us through and through. Show me how to partner with you in this process.

Chapter 7

Core Messages

Several days after our last meeting I got a call from Will. He indicated that the whole matter at work preoccupied his mind. With 20/20 hindsight he could see how poorly he had handled the encounter with his co-workers. Nothing else had happened in the workplace and everyone was "business as usual," but as he reassessed the conflict he began to feel more shame than blame. I suggested that he come and pick me up for lunch. That way, once we were done, we could go back to my office to chat further.

Meeting 3

(During lunch)

Will: *I will have to admit that I underestimated the power of the flesh. As I look back I really think that I have been trying to mold my flesh to live up to what I consider Biblical standards rather than depend solely on Christ to mold me for His glory.*

Matt: I completely understand. That was my story for years. Now, even though I know better, I find myself falling back into that trap.

Will: *The thing is I am getting a picture of what I am doing wrong, but I really don't know what it looks like to handle it differently.*

Matt: Will, that is where we are moving. We have a couple of other diagnostic steps to take before we dive into the solution… which of course is found in our hope in Christ alone.

(Having finished lunch, Will and Matt are back at Matt's office)

Will: *As I said to you on the phone, I've been really struggling with what happened at the office a week ago. I am having a hard time figuring out whether God is trying to get my attention or I am just obsessing over this whole thing. You asked a question at our first lunch… something about whether what I was feeling was familiar to me, well… that has stayed with me.*

Matt: I can tell this has been difficult, but it seems God is up to something. What about that last question? Are these feelings familiar?

Will: *I thought I was past all of this!*

Matt: Past what?

Will: *It's ridiculous.*

Matt: Will, nothing is ridiculous. You know you are safe sharing with me. Have you ever shared whatever is on your mind with anybody else before now?

Will: *No! I have always just considered it kid stuff and unimportant. But I can now see that it might be deeper than that. Those feelings are very familiar. Inside, whenever someone questions my decisions in any way, I take it totally as a personal slam and it hurts me. Sometimes I am able to cover it up. But sometimes when I feel that way, whatever I do next does not turn out well. I either emotionally close down giving people the impression that I am mad or aloof or I say something that, as hard as I try to say it nicely, comes out defensive or combative. Certain people really seem to push that button. At times I have felt they mean to. But even then I should be patient and non-defensive. Usually after it's all over, I realize I am being too sensitive and they are not intending to attack me. But it sure feels like they are when it's happening. It comes out in other ways as well. I am extremely competitive in certain areas… so much so that I stoop to envy when others are honored in areas that are important to me… even my friends. The other thing that drives me crazy is my perfectionist tendencies in certain areas. I must get it right… I must do it perfectly! Even my wife jumps me for this stuff.*

Matt: When did you first notice it?

Will: *Which part?*

Matt: The feeling that someone is questioning your competence.

Will: (Emotions starting to set in) *When I was a little kid.*

Matt: What did that look like?

Will: *Don't get me wrong here… I have great parents! Man, were they patient with me, and I know that I must have given them fits. My brother was a straight A superstar student. Let's just say that I was far from that. It didn't really get bad until I was in the eighth grade. My parents moved me from my public school environment to a true college prep school that my brother attended. That year was a disaster! I remember one of my eighth grade teachers meeting with me and my parents and telling them that I had made the lowest grade she had ever had in her class. She shared that she did not*

	know how it was possible, even if someone had not attended class, to make that low a grade.
Matt:	That hurt! What do you think was going on?
Will:	*I don't really know. This I do know, whether it was severe immaturity, or some other form of preoccupation… or ADD, ADHD, or some other type of childhood learning challenge, or (emotions grow)…*
Matt:	How do you think the current issues are related to this story in your past?
Will:	*Well, I flunked the eighth grade and my parents moved me to another private school in the area and I did all right. But I was still never a great student. Then I went to college and crammed about a quarter and a half of work into a two-year period. Needless to say, that wasn't going anywhere. So I went out into the business world at my parent's advice. It was good advice. It was at this point that I began to notice a lot of sensitivity when people questioned me or my work ethic.*
Matt:	So you are connecting your experience when you were in middle school through college with what happened the other day?
Will:	*I guess deep inside I am very sensitive about any level of failure, but particularly in some areas that I now pride myself in. I guess I have been striving ever since those early years to prove something.*
Matt:	Prove what?
Will:	*Maybe that I am not dumb… that I can follow through on things… that I am not a failure. Since then I have graduated from college with high grades, been very successful in business, speak for conventions in my industry, serve on the board for several businesses, and even wrote a few well-received books. I'm obviously not saying this to impress you… not that I am not capable of that. I am saying this because it's never enough. It's never good enough.*
Matt:	When you were a kid, and you had these academic challenges, how did it make you feel?
Will:	(Emotions heighten… quiet tears) *Embarrassed… real embarrassed. Like everybody knew. I felt shame.*

(The room becomes quiet. Will sat momentarily pondering his situation.)

Will:	*My two co-workers approached me with critiques and ideas on improving our practices at work and I just reacted. I was defensive. No wonder they were irritated. I felt personally attacked. She was right. I wasn't listening. Just plain defensive. Here I am nearly 40 years old, and I act like a little child.*
Matt:	So this chase to prove you are competent, without even being aware of it, became a central focus in your life. Your perceived success in this area is a

major source of your identity.

Will: *You just don't know… and I can see how it's eating me up. It ate me up when I was a kid when I really did feel incompetent and it's got me now. Today, if anyone… my wife, kids, boss, co-workers… anyone I respect or care about, in a kidding manner or serious manner, criticize or critique an area that I am responsible for, a screaming alarm goes off to protect me. I hate this about myself.*

Summary 4- Core Messages

Fortunately many people experience supportive and encouraging core messages that shape their lives. Unfortunately, as a result of the fallen nature of man, every person lives with core messages that also negatively contribute to fleshly foundational beliefs, whether they were intended or just perceived that way. In Will's life this was true. Core messages (perception of significant experiences) contributed to a powerful belief that he was incompetent. Early in his life these messages created painful embarrassment and shame. As time went on, he developed a belief that he was incompetent. All people have significant experiences that strongly contribute to their fleshly foundational beliefs. These messages, whether intended by others or not, are powerful.

Will created a set of personal standards that must be met to overcome this sense of indictment. Anytime he felt he was not living up to these performance standards or someone challenged his success, he reacted inwardly if not outwardly as well. Again, think back with me to the second chapter on the fall of man. We are born disconnected from God. At birth we are starving for what we were created to be, but without connection to the creator who is the only true source. We find ourselves empty of true intimacy, identity, and influence. Each person goes about life creating their own straw systems of belief to prove they are lovable, unique, and purposeful.

These beliefs serve as a base of beliefs to process self-image (pride). They serve as primary standards for hopes of experiencing self-love, self-identity, and self-worth. The only true result is further emptiness, emitting egotistical pride, insecurity, and insignificance. This insane chase, the desperation and turmoil, are all about the loss, the cavern that separates man from the only source of true fulfillment. People are famished for communion with their Maker and the flood of intimacy, identity, and influence that is its overflow. The straw system that Will built and tried to constantly prop up had always been broken, and now it was coming to light. As hard as it is to face these realities, it is a wonderful step forward to solely depend upon Christ and re-engage with His intimacy, identity, and influence.

Even after years of self-effort, in spite of Will proving himself by any normal societal standards to be successful and competent, the result was exhausting and never-ending. His source of joy was dependent upon fulfilling the beliefs and standards derived from his straw system.

Think about it!

1. Does it surprise you that core messages had such impact in Will's life?

2. What are common examples of core messages in our society?

3. What experiences contributed core messages into your life, both good and bad?

Caution!

Recommendation: If this exercise creates great pain or you recognize you are currently dealing with depression, please seek a highly trained friend or professional counsel to support you in your study.

Meeting 3 with Will continues...

Matt: Core messages are powerful in our life. At the root of your fleshly foundational belief (incompetence is not an option) are significant experiences that have created core messages from your past. These perceptions constantly contribute to your thought process, feelings, and on a deeper level, your identity. The only method outside of Christ to fight these perceived messages is to jump through more hoops and work harder or to prove the messenger wrong. In your case, in spite of you proving yourself as very competent by any normal standards, years later, you continue to battle this fear. This is the spin of despair.

Will: *Spin of despair... that is exactly how I feel.*

Matt: I often spin in my emotion as well… and it isn't any fun. Let me show you a graph that will help you process the challenge you face.

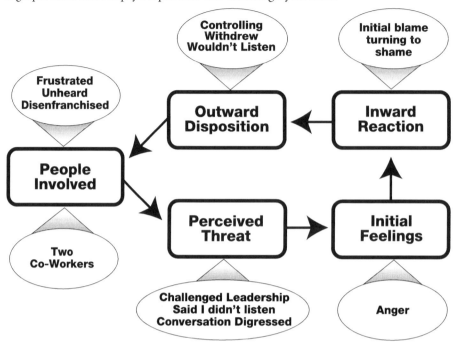

Matt: Notice first of all you can see "people involved" on the left. In your case this was the two co-workers.

Will: *That's right.*

Matt: Then you can see "perceived threat." What do you think the perceived threat was? In other words, in what way did you feel threatened?

Will: *I felt that they were challenging my leadership. They seemed frustrated the longer we talked. They said that I didn't listen.*

Matt: And what were your initial feelings?

Will: *I was angry.*

Matt: Your anger birthed inward emotions of blame. A week later the anger turned more toward shame.

Will: *I felt my co-workers were questioning my competence. This pushed a button in me, one that always sets off an alarm.*

Matt: And then how did you respond outwardly?

Will: *I cut the meeting short. I got controlling and withdrew… wouldn't listen.*

Matt: How did they leave feeling?

Will: *Frustrated, unheard, and probably disenfranchised.*

Matt: It certainly feels like your two co-workers are the central problem, but I think that they were mostly the catalyst for this painful experience. The real problem relates to a deeper issue… your fleshly foundational belief. The spin of despair is a result of this belief that you must prove yourself through being fully competent. I am excited that you don't have to continue on this crazy spin. Christ will rescue you! Look at the following graph that shows the spin.

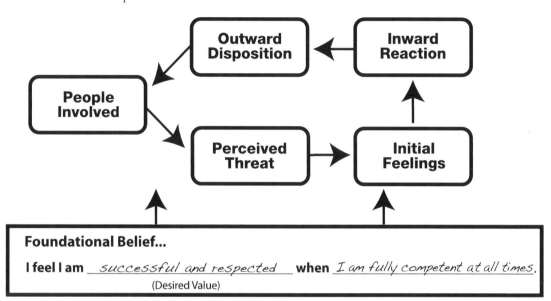

Will: *Makes total sense.*

Matt: Notice the fleshly foundational belief is at the base of your challenge. As we said, your base issue is proving yourself by being fully competent. These fleshly beliefs only cause pain. What I want to share with you is a Biblical way to approach these beliefs… with supernatural power to change you from the inside out. I hope that the process helps you, but the power is not in the process but in Christ. We are moving in a good direction…getting away from the spin and moving toward Christ. The following graph now shows where we are in the process.

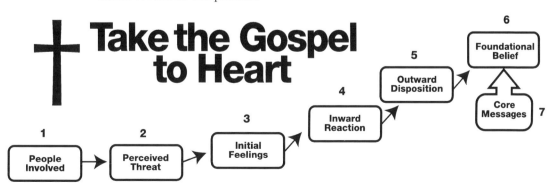

Please fill out the following Core Messages Worksheet.

Core Messages

What have been the "core messages" that have shaped your "foundational beliefs?"

People

① Who was the messenger?

What was the message?

What was the impact?

② Who was the messenger?

What was the message?

What was the impact?

Experiences

① What was the experience?

What was the message from the experience?

What was the impact?

② What was the experience?

What was the message from the experience?

What was the impact?

Only Through Jesus Christ!

Jesus Christ provides for you the solution to your dilemma, the clarity to your perplexity, and the answer yielding peace for your desperation. Through Him you can be free from fear of punishment, free to live a life of righteousness, and blessed with full assurance of eternal life. Through Christ, the once-severed relationship with Jehovah God is reunited. Life will erupt within your once spiritually dead heart. The rivers of intimacy will be free to flow. The Father again will delight in you and you will bask in His rich love. Futility is spoiled with eternal purpose.

The Spirit of the Lord is on Me, because He has anointed Me to preach good news to the poor. He has sent Me to proclaim freedom for the prisoners and recovery of sight for the blind, to release the oppressed, to proclaim the year of the Lord's favor. Then He rolled up the scroll, gave it back to the attendant and sat down. The eyes of everyone in the synagogue were fastened on Him. "Today this scripture is fulfilled in your hearing." (Luke 4: 18 – 21)

There could not have been sweeter words for those who were desperately anticipating the fulfillment of the promise from years gone by (Isaiah 61). Today, to those who are enchanted with the worldly chase and its promised plunder, this promise of hope is unimpressive and useless. To those who find their hope in arrogant religious ritual, this promise is threatening. But if you are one who is empty and hungry, who is desperately perplexed… the prisoner, the blind, and the oppressed…this good news could not be better.

It is from the perplexed and desperate vantage point that one is most capable of clearly focusing on very real hope. If you are screaming for true freedom, sight, and release, hope is here. His name is Jesus. (I Peter 2: 24) Your heart-cry is typical of those who he touches!

- How about the government official whose son was deathly ill? Jesus healed his son. How desperate was he? (John 4: 46 -53)

- How about Peter's mother-in-law? He saw her sick with a fever and she was healed. How desperate was she? (Matthew 8: 14, 15)

- How about the two men at the tomb possessed by demons that were so violent that no one could even come near them? Jesus had compassion on them and drove the demons into the pigs nearby. How desperate were they? (Matthew 8: 28 – 33)

- How about the paralytic who was carried by his friends to Jesus on a mat? He forgave his sins and then healed his body. How desperate was he? (Matthew 9: 2 – 8)

- How about the invalid who had gone back and forth to the healing pool in Bethesda for 38 years? Jesus told him to get up and walk, and he did. How desperate was he? (John 5: 2 – 8)

- How about the widow whose son was already dead in the coffin? Jesus touched the coffin and the son rose from the dead. How desperate were they? (Luke 7: 12 – 16)

- How about the woman who had suffered with a problem with bleeding for over 12 years? Jesus miraculously healed her. How desperate was she? (Luke 8: 43 – 48)

- Even from within the possessed man in the synagogue, the demons knew that Jesus was the "Holy one of God," and they were cast out and the man was set free. How desperate was he? (Luke 4:31 – 36)

Christ Alone!

Jesus makes a bleeding woman well. He makes paralyzed people walk. He makes blind men see. He makes disease disappear. He makes demons flee. He makes dead men rise. He cannot be contained by men. He cannot be restrained by demons. He cannot be retained by Satan himself. Sin cannot befall him. Death cannot triumph over Him. Storms do not disturb him and the winds and the sea, they obey him. He rules over nature.

His dominion is eternal. His existence is everlasting and His Lordship is unmistakable. Nothing confuses Him. Nothing thwarts Him. Nothing frustrates Him. Nothing masters Him. Nothing prevails over Him. His knowledge is infinite. His presence is universal. His power is without limits. He is exalted in the heavenly. He is master of all powers. He is the Alpha and Omega, the Beginning and the End. He is the Divine One, the Son of God. He is the Savior. His life mastered perfection. On the cross He conquered sin.

Through His resurrection He defeated death. For those guilty, He has justified. For the enemy, He has reconciled. For those enslaved He has redeemed. For those condemned, He has atoned. For those eternally damned, He has glorified. He is hope in despair. He is a companion to the lonely, security for the fearful, purpose for the aimless, strength to the weak, light in the darkness; He is a master, brother, lover, and friend. He is the real deal.

No one can be spiritually satisfied with fleshly solutions. Without God's intervention, the only solution man has is temporal and superficial. We do not need a plastic surgeon; we need a heart surgeon who is able to transform the very heart of man. The heart of man is "deceitful above all things and beyond cure." (Jeremiah 17: 9) It is out of touch with God with no recourse. (Isaiah 59:2) It is spiritually dead. (Romans 6:23a)

Jesus came for the desperate. Jesus came to not only speak the Good News, but to deliver and secure the Good News. "But God demonstrated his love for us in this; while we were still sinners, Christ died for us." (Romans 5: 8) By God's grace man has been provided a way of escape. Man is left with a choice: He can receive Jesus Christ and trust him alone for salvation, or he can reject this wonderful gift. The Bible teaches that everyone who believes in Him receives forgiveness for sins through His name. (John 1: 12) Christ's redemptive work truly sets believers free.

Through Christ we have confidence that we will spend eternity with Him. We are fully pleasing to God. We are totally accepted by God.

What an incredible message! Jesus is the answer. In Him we will become God's living portrait to proclaim hope. We can experience His unsearchable riches and make plain to everyone the great work of Christ.

Praise the Name of Jesus!

Passage:

John 10:10

The thief comes only to steal and kill and destroy; I cam that they may have life, and have it abundantly.

Praise:

Jesus, you are the way, the truth, and the life. Thank you for your abundance.

Ponder:

Remember a time when you saw the abundance of God. Celebrate what God did for you.

Pray:

Jesus, thank you that you don't deal in scarcity. You didn't come to give us just enough to get by. Thank you for the richness, the depth, and the splendor of the life we have in you. Help me to live each day with a mindset of abundance rather than want.

Chapter 8

The Power of The Cross!

The following week when Will and I met together he came in frustrated. Within a couple of minutes we moved from small talk to what was on his mind. The night before he and his wife (Jenn) had a blow-up. It was over money. He was looking into their checking account and realized that she had written several checks beyond the current balance in the account. Fortunately, they did have their account connected to their savings so the fee was small, but this whole situation totally irritated him. He pointed out her mistake in a huff. He felt she dismissed it and did not take it seriously. As a result he proceeded from being irritated to becoming condemning and controlling. He threatened to take her name off the account if she couldn't behave. Jenn reacted in anger, calling him an insensitive, controlling bully.

Meeting 4 with Will.

Will: *So that's what happened last night. She does frustrate the heck out of me sometimes. I just can't understand why she doesn't get the importance of this.*

Matt: How did it end?

Will: *I followed her around from room to room trying to get my point across and she finally locked the bedroom door and I slept on the couch. What had been a quiet evening with the family exploded into angry discourse leaving Jenn hurt and the children upset and me feeling misunderstood. I woke up this morning feeling totally frustrated. While I was still irritated with her, I was particularly frustrated with myself. I was a jerk! This whole situation feels like it revolves around the same area we've been discussing.*

Matt: What do you mean?

Will: *I have been praying that I would quit acting on my fleshly foundational beliefs since we identified several of them a few weeks ago. It just doesn't seem to be working. Most of what happened last night is about my issues. I preached at her, talked down at her like a little girl and followed her around like an attorney making my point until she finally had as much as she could take and shut me out.*

Matt: How do you associate this episode with your fleshly foundational beliefs?

Will: *Anytime I don't feel in control of our finances I lose it. This is one of the areas that I pride myself in. When I was in college and early in marriage I treated my finances with the same immaturity and carelessness that I did my school work. On several occasions I made a big mess and bounced some checks on my account. I had to deal with the banker who was a friend of my parents. That was painful.*

Matt: You mean the bounced check fees?

Will: *That was bad… but not half as bad as the feeling of being lectured and scolded by the banker. I am sure that because of the friendship with my parents, and probably interest in me, he took extra liberty to straighten me out. It felt just like I was sitting in that classroom in the eighth grade hearing my teacher talk about me hopelessly.*

Matt: I can see that. So with regard to your money, you decided that nothing like that would ever happen again. You were not going to go through the pain of embarrassment and shame that comes from incompetence. In your mind, this was one of those areas that you put on your list that could not be compromised.

Will: *Absolutely!*

Matt: And when Jenn botched up the checkbook you reacted. I know she must care.

Will: *She does, but not when I go into my "holier than thou" preacher/prosecuting attorney mode. She just shuts down.*

Matt: You think? (little sarcasm intended) How do you think she feels when you do that?

Will: *Awful! Like a scolded child with no hope.*

Matt: Does that sound familiar?

Will: *What do you mean?*

Matt: Before I make my point, I am very thankful that you are beginning to understand what happened last night and that you care about what she feels. Don't miss the importance of how far you have come in understanding your challenge. But there is a very interesting correlation I'd like to make. We tend to cast judgment and communicate our displeasure out of our pain, and we don't even know it. You were using the very thing that strikes fear into your own heart as your artillery to scold her and control her… embarrassment and shame.

Matt continues: (tears welling up in Will's eyes) I am certainly not trying to be insensitive or mean, but we all do this. What is in our heart flows out, even the things that we would never want to communicate. I hope that isn't too bold for me to say.

Will: *No, no… don't apologize. The point is well taken and totally true. She probably has no idea why I treat her that way. Unfortunately, I am pretty sure that whenever I feel threatened, this is the way that I fight. In this case, I became the bully. Matt, can I take a minute and go outside to make a call to Jenn?*

Matt: Sure.

1. Do you think that Will has made progress in understanding his fleshly foundational beliefs? If so, in what ways?

2. In this particular episode mentioned in this chapter, who was affected by his struggle?

3. How did he react to his wife's oversight regarding the checking account?

4. Explain why you think he scolded her by attempting to use embarrassment and shame?

5. When you are acting out of fleshly foundational beliefs toward others, what is the typical method you use to make your point?

Observation:

Will had come a long way since our first conversation. He clearly understands the spin of despair that has victimized him. He realizes he can't do it in his own power and he must have utter dependence upon Christ. But how does this really work? Many who get to this point stall as a result of not knowing how to practice living in the power of the gospel... Take the Gospel to Heart. Will faces this critical step immediately in front of him.

(A few minutes later Will returns)

Will: *Okay, I don't know if that made total sense to her, but she knows that I know I was a jerk and am very sorry. I asked her if we could talk more about it tonight.*

Matt: Good for you! Today we are turning the corner from diagnosing the spin of despair to trusting Christ for our daily victory. I want to make sure that the pathway to victory becomes crystal clear. This is the really good stuff! We are moving from diagnosis of the problem to the solution. We will now see how to take our fleshly foundational beliefs to the cross to find deep inner cleansing, freedom and life-changing power. Look at the following graph showing where we are in the process.

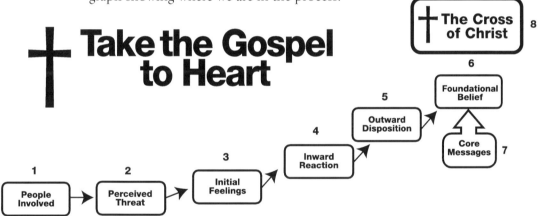

Matt continues: Let's briefly review. Colossians 2: 6 says…"*So then, just as you received Christ Jesus as Lord, continue to live in him.*" According to this passage, if we could go back to how we initially received Christ, we could find the answer to how to live in his power. Will, when you initially accepted Christ, what was your part in the process?

Will: *I had to accept Him into my life.*

Matt: Agreed, it was an act of your will. But even the faith by which you responded came from where?

Will: *It came from Him.*

Matt: I agree! You were completely responsible for your sin, but only He could save you. The secret to your daily walk is no different than the hope you originally found in Christ years ago. Your only hope for salvation was centered in Christ alone and your only hope for spiritual growth and maturity is also centered in Christ alone. Except for His great work, you are helpless. Your only hope for daily victory is dependence upon Him.

Will: *Definitely!*

Matt: Are you sure that you are at the end of your own effort and have no other avenues to pursue victory on you own? [1]

Will: *I am positive. I have thrown in the towel.*

Matt: That is good.

Will: *At first it felt terrible like I was defeated. But I am beginning to sense the peace and strength that is following by trusting Him alone. But it is such a battle.*

Matt: The reason that it is bringing peace and strength is that you are experiencing Christ-centered brokenness, not hopelessness. I am reminded of Psalm 51: 17. It says…"The sacrifices of God are a broken spirit; a broken and contrite heart, O God, you will not despise." This is how we originally began in Christ. We were dead! That is as broken and contrite as you can get. We were totally dependent upon Him for saving us and that is how we will find the answers now… from a broken position and totally dependent. Your choices are limited. You can keep moving along with the same fleshly foundational beliefs and suffer the consequences or can turn to Christ. Christ's work on the cross will bring power and victory.

Will: *Obviously I want the work of Christ and his power and victory.*

Matt: It's going to take a couple of minutes of concentration, but please read aloud the following promises resulting from the work of Christ on the cross. These passages and promises are the foundation for your Christ-centered beliefs and identity. Of course all of the promises that result from the cross are necessities in our life. But what we are looking for today are the particular promises that speak to your current need. What was your fleshly foundational belief that we discovered?

Will: *That I am successful only when I am fully competent in my own eyes as well as others.*

Matt: Will, please look over the following questions and pick out Christ's promises that seem to speak directly to your fleshly foundational belief. It could be more than one.

Instructions to reader: Please carefully read through the incredible promises that result from the work of Christ on the cross (The Gospel). Examine each beautiful facet carefully and then answer the questions that follow. Like Will, pick out the aspects of the gospel that speak directly to your fleshly foundational belief. Will's fleshly foundational belief was... *I am successful only when I am fully competent in my own eyes as well as others.*

What is yours?

Fleshly Foundational Belief:

✝ Promises of The Cross

Our tendency is to run quickly past wording like "the power and promises of the cross." Many believers would say they are familiar with the idea and get it. But the truth is, most of us pay little attention to these promises and simply "do our best" trying to live the Christian life. What a terrible loss! The truth related with Christ's redemptive power and promises yielded through His work on the cross are the living sustenance that provides us supernatural life and victory. The apostle Paul certainly viewed it this way...

"For I resolved to know nothing while I was with you except Jesus Christ and Him crucified." I Corinthians 2:2

We are Justified

Romans 5:1

"Therefore, since we have been justified through faith, we have peace with God through our Lord Jesus Christ."

Definition of justified: to be declared not guilty, to clear the record, acquittal.

When we accepted Christ into our life, we accepted that His death on the cross completely satisfied the debt for our sins and we were declared not guilty. Our record is wiped clean. We now enjoy being completely forgiven and fully pleasing to God.

Promise: You are fully pleasing to God!

Because you are justified you are "fully pleasing" to God. This means he...

How does being "fully pleasing" to God affect your view of God?

How does it affect your view of yourself?

How should it change your general mindset about life?

We are Reconciled

Colossians 1:22

"But now He has reconciled you by Christ's physical body through death to present you holy in His sight, without blemish, and free from accusation."

Definition of reconciled: to be brought back into a right relationship with someone.

When we accepted Christ into our life, we accepted that His death on the cross put us into a perfect relationship with Him. We were enemies of God, but now we are His children.

Promise: You are totally loved and accepted by God!

Because you are reconciled, you are totally loved and accepted by God.
This means he…

How does being "loved and accepted" by God affect your view of God?

How does it affect your view of yourself?

How should it change your general mindset about life?

We are "at one" with God (Atoned)

I John 4:9-10

"This is how God showed his love among us: He sent his one and only Son into the world that we might live through Him. This is love: not that we loved God, but that He loved us and sent his Son as an atoning sacrifice for our sins."

Definition of atoning sacrifice: a sacrifice that completely satisfies.

When we accepted Christ into our life, we accepted that His death on the cross was the perfect sacrifice and completely satisfied God's holy requirement. We were once under God's wrath for our sin, but we now have no reason to fear punishment. Because of Christ's atoning sacrifice, God is completely satisfied, and we are made "at one" with Him.

Promise: You are free from the fear of punishment from God!

Because you are "atoned for" you are free from the fear of punishment from God. This means he…

How does being "free from the fear of punishment" of God affect your view of God?

How does it affect your view of yourself? How should it change your general mindset about life?

We are Redeemed

Ephesians 5:1

"In Him we have redemption through His blood, the forgiveness of sins, in accordance with the riches of God's grace."

Definition of redemption: to buy one's freedom back from slavery.

When we accepted Christ into our life, we accepted that His death on the cross would pay the complete debt for our sin. We were slaves to sin, but we are now free to live a life of righteousness through Christ.

Promise: You are no longer a slave to sin, but set free to live a life of righteousness!

Because you are redeemed you are no longer a slave to sin, but set free to live a life of righteousness. This means he…

How does being "set free to live a life of righteousness" affect your view of God?

How does it affect your view of yourself?

How should it change your general mindset about life?

We are Sanctified (also being)

I Thessalonians 5: 23

"May God himself, the God of peace, sanctify you through and through. May your whole spirit, soul and body be kept blameless at the coming of our Lord Jesus Christ."

Definition of sanctification: to set apart for God, make holy…positional sanctification: (I Cor. 1: 12)

At salvation, through Christ, the believer is set apart by the Holy Spirit with imputed righteousness and life.

Progressive sanctification: (I Thessalonians 5: 23) The continued work of Christ through the Holy Spirit in the believer which sets him apart for God in his experience eliminating sin and producing Christ's fruit.

Promise: You can fully depend on Christ for your spiritual development!

Because you are being sanctified (progressive), you can fully depend on Christ for your spiritual development. This means he…

How does the assurance that you can "fully depend on Christ for your spiritual development" affect your view of God?

How does it affect your view of yourself?

We are Adopted (given the right of sonship)

Galatians 4: 3 – 7

³"So also, when we were children, we were in slavery under the basic principles of the world. ⁴But when the time had fully come, God sent His Son, born of a woman, born under law, ⁵to redeem those under law, that we might receive the full rights of sons. ⁶Because you are sons, God sent the Spirit of His Son into our hearts, the Spirit who calls out, "Abba, Father." ⁷So you are no longer a slave, but a son; and since you are a son, God has made you also an heir."

Definition of adoption: to legally be taken into one's family and raised as one's own child.

When we accepted Christ into our life, we accepted that His death on the cross would secure our privilege of sonship to God, being adopted into His family with full rights. This gift provides all privileges of a son including closeness, affection and generosity, which are at the heart of the relationship. To be right with God the Judge is a great thing, but to be loved and cared for by God the Father is greater. (J.I. Packer - *Knowing God*)

Promise: You are a beloved child of God!

Because you are adopted, you are a beloved child of God. This means he…

How does being "a beloved child of God" affect your view of God?

How does it affect your view of yourself?

How should it change your general mindset about life?

We have been uniquely created with Purpose

I Peter 2: 9 - 10

⁹But you are a chosen people, a royal priesthood, a holy nation, a people belonging to God, that you may declare the praises of Him who called you out of darkness into his wonderful light." (Also Hebrews 12: 1)

Definition of created with purpose: When we accepted Christ into our life, we accepted that His death on the cross set us free to use our uniquely endowed gifts, talents, and personalities for His glory. (Psalm 139: 13 -16).

Promise: You are uniquely created with value and purpose to make a specific difference for His glory!

Because you are uniquely created with value and purpose, you can make a specific difference for His glory. This means he…

How does being "making a specific difference for His glory" affect your view of God?

How does it affect your view of yourself?

How should it change your general mindset about life?

We will be Glorified

Romans 8:30

"And those He predestined, He also called; those He called, He also justified; those He justified, He also glorified."

Definition of glorification: a state of eternal blessedness believers enter at death.

When we accepted Christ into our life, we accepted that His death and resurrection guaranteed an eternally blessed existence with Him. We were eternally damned and destined for hell, but we now have confidence that we will spend eternity in heaven.

Promise: You have full assurance of eternal life with God!

Because you will be glorified you can have full assurance of eternal life with God. This means he…

How does being "fully assured of eternal life with God" affect your view of God?

How does it affect your view of yourself?

How should it change your general mindset about life?

Summing it Up!

The cross satisfied every righteous requirement of God to spiritually restore man. The work of Christ was for one purpose… To redeem man for God's glory. This incredible act of love redeemed man from a broken relationship with God restoring a uniquely personal relationship. Through the work of Christ man moved from being God's enemy to becoming God's beloved child. What a great price Christ paid, but what a great blessing we received! Before this redemptive work, we were dead in sin. We had hearts of stone… not even a pang of spiritual hope. But Christ died that we might truly live. We have been given new live and new identity through Christ.

"[4]But because of His great love for us, God, who is rich in mercy, [5]made us alive with Christ even when we were dead in transgressions–it is by grace you have been saved. [6]And God raised us up with Christ and seated us with Him in the heavenly realms in Christ Jesus, [7]in order that in the coming ages He might show the incomparable riches of His grace, expressed in His kindness to us in Christ Jesus. [8]For it is by grace you have been saved, through faith–and this is not from yourselves, it is the gift of God– [9]not by works, so that no one can boast. [10]For we are God's handiwork, created in Christ Jesus to do good works, which God prepared in advance for us to do." Ephesians 2: 4–10

Please fill in the following worksheet to clearly identify how your old fleshly foundational beliefs are affected by the work of Christ on the cross for you.

Promises of the Cross

Please read the list of promises resulting from Christ's work on the cross.

We are Justified (Romans 5:1)
Definition of justified: to be declared not guilty, to clear the record, acquittal.
We are full pleasing to God!

We are Reconciled (Colossians 1:22)
Definition of reconciled: to be brought back into a right relationship with someone.
We are totally loved and accepted by God!

We are "at one" with God (Atoned) (1 John 4:9-10)
Definition of atoning sacrifice: a sacrifice that completely satisfies.
We are "at one" and free from the fear of punishment from God!

We are Redeemed (Ephesians 5:1)
Definition of redemption: to buy one's freedom back from slavery.
We are set free to live a life of righteousness!

We are Sanctified (also being) (1 Corinthians 1:12; 1 Thessalonians 5:23)
Definition of Sanctification: to set apart for God, makes holy… Positional and Progressive
We can fully depend on Christ for our spiritual development!

We are Adopted (given the right of Sonship): (Galatians 4:3-7)
Definition of Adoption: to legally be taken into one's family and raised as one's own child.
We are true sons of God!

We have been created with Purpose (1 Peter 2:9-10; Hebrews 12:1)
Definition: Uniquely created with purpose… given gifts, talents, personalities, calling
We are created to make a difference for His glory!

We will be Glorified (Romans 8:30)
Definition of glorification: a state of eternal blessedness believers enter at death
We have full assurance of eternal life with God!

List each primary "foundational belief" from the prior page and then the promise and application that most applies.

Foundational Belief	Promise	New Christ-centered Belief

Foundational Belief	Promise	New Christ-centered Belief

Passage:

1 John 3:1

See what great love the Father has lavished on us, that we should be called children of God! And that is what we are!

Praise:

Worship God as Father. Tell him what it means to you to be his child.

Ponder:

Ask God to remind you of the many ways he has lavished his love on you.

Pray:

Father, thank you that I am your child. What a privilege! What an honor! May that truth permeate down deep into the depth of my core and be the fiber through which I see myself and others.

Chapter 9

The Power of The Cross! (Part 2)

Conversation 4:

Will: *A lot of this information about the cross sounds familiar to me, but I'm not sure I really dwell on it much.*

Matt: That is the goal… to "take every thought captive" through the beauty of the cross. These Biblical truths share the relational freedom you and I are starving for. We all struggle allowing our fleshly identity to bully us. This is a case of mistake identity. Christ has given us a new identity. On the previous worksheet which promises seem to directly apply to your fleshly foundational beliefs?

Will: *There are several that particularly apply. But I think being reconciled and adopted as a true son are the most obvious ones… to be totally loved and accepted by God. But I am not sure how it directly applies to my thoughts, attitudes, and actions?*

Matt: Great question! Let's consider a story to answer that question… one that you will catch onto fairly quickly from scripture. Pretend for a minute that you were a king's son who had everything. He not only provided for your physical needs but passionately loved you. One day you had the audacity to ask your dad for money before hightailing it out of town for your own pleasure. You squandered everything like the fool you were. One day, in the pit of despair and emptiness, you realized your foolish ways and were fully aware of your stupidity and defiance. You knew that you deserved nothing from your dad, but you also knew that even the lowliest servants at your home were physically taken care of better than you were. So you headed home, in a state of repentance, in hope that somehow your dad would have at least a tiny bit of empathy and allow you to become one of his servants. Now, as you were approaching home you could see tearing out of the front gate someone running toward you. You recognized it was your dad. Before you could even react he had taken you into his arms, holding and hugging you with tears of elation and celebration. He joyously danced around you without care for what others might think. Your dad escorted you to the palace as he sang for joy… my son is home… my son is home! A celebration erupted and you were blessed and loved like only a dad can love his own son. You were treated, not as you deserved to be treated, but as the son that you were.

Will: *Good story! Wonder who came up with it? (Fun sarcasm intended) Wow! God's unconditional love is unbelievable.*

Matt: It is! You are a son… His son! So how does that affect your heart-cry for approval?

Will: *Man… (Will pauses, a bit bewildered)*

Matt: If it's hard to apply, think about the prodigal son in the story and what effect his dad's love and acceptance had on him. God loves you like that! How could that knowledge change your perspective?

Will: *Well, the prodigal experienced his father's unconditional love and acceptance. He had no need to prove himself. He had nothing.*

Matt: What about you? If that knowledge was your new foundation of belief, how would that affect your old "fleshly foundational belief"… that approval is given when you are fully competent?

Will: *My competence wouldn't be connected to whether I have approval. In Christ I would already be approved. That's the starting point. I would sense security in His arms. I wouldn't always be trying to prove myself. It would allow me to work with sincere motives instead of selfish motives.*

Matt: How would your viewpoint of your "core messages" change? How would they be different?

Will:	*If I really knew that God loved and accepted me like that I would no longer find my identity in myself, but in Him, I would hope that I could forgive those that might have hurt me. People's input in general would be filtered through a secure person rather than a defensive person.*
Matt:	And what would happen to your "inward reaction"… blame and shame?
Will:	*I would not be an armed bomb ready to explode at the least amount of challenge. Because my base of hope would be found in God's love only, I wouldn't be overly sensitive and there would be no need for blame or shame. I would feel pleased with input. There would be no negative feeling of shame following the meeting.*
Matt:	You're really getting this!
Will:	*I know. I wish that I could "really" believe it!*
Matt:	You do and you will more and more. How would your understanding of this unconditional love and acceptance from God affect your "initial feeling" of anger?
Will:	*There would be no anger because there is nothing telling me from within that I am an incompetent bum. I would show appreciation for people's input.*
Matt:	What about your "perceived threats"… how would they be seen if you could look through these eyes of being loved and accepted?
Will:	*I would digest challenges with wisdom and not have them polluted with all of my insecurity. I could hear critique and act on it wisely. I could even hear criticism and rather than react, be open and receiving. Now that would be a miracle!*
Matt:	God's into miracles you know. And then finally, what about "people involved"… your two co-workers? How would they be affected?
Will:	*Not just them! How about my wife and my kids and my friends? Think of the times that I could have made a powerful impact for Christ in their lives, but I was only caught up in my selfish trap. My co-workers and I would have probably had a profitable conversation, grown in respect, and we would have achieved better teamwork. Last night I could have lovingly had a discussion with my wife rather than bully her. You know, this whole fleshly straw system that I built pierces every aspect of life. It's a killer!*
Matt:	Will, don't let this spiral into a sense of blame and shame. It seems that there is genuine conviction coming from Christ. I want to compare the old flesh response to your new response based upon the gospel. Take a look at this comparison.

Flesh Response		**Trusting Christ**	
People Involved	Two co-workers - Initiate conversation with concern and critique	**People Involved**	Two co-workers - Initiate conversation with concern and critique
Perceived Threat	Challenged leadership said I didn't listen conversation digressed	**Perceived Threat**	Would view conversation with wisdom/hear critique/ act on it wisely/ could hear criticism and be open and receiving
Initial Feeling	Anger	**Initial Feeling**	Wecome input
Inward Reaction	Blame and later shame	**Inward Reaction**	Show appreciation for input
Outward Disposition	Controlling/ withdrew/ wouldn't listen	**Outward Disposition**	Welcomed critique/ showed interest/ listened carefully/ appreciative
Foundational Belief	I feel I am successful and respected when I am fully compentent at all times	**Foundational Belief**	I am secure in the fact that I am unconditionally loved and accepted by God. Other's perspective is helpful for the purpose of wise counsel, accountability and critique
Core Messages	Feeling like I need to constantly prove competence/shame/ embarrassment often on the surface of emotions	**Core Messages**	Could forgive unwise input from past/ could learn helpful advice
People Involved	Two co-workers - frustrated, unheard, disenfranchised	**People Involved**	Two co-workers - profitable conversation, grown in respect, and better team work

Vs.

Straw System Implodes Christ Glorified

Will: *Christ's work is not only powerful but it's practical. That's a cool list. That brings it all together. The problem is I am still skeptical about anything really changing for the long haul.*

Matt: I completely understand. Whatever you do, don't forget who rescues you… it is Christ alone! You can't do it but He will. Let's review a minute:

- He initially saved you

- He has given you heart surgery and supernaturally taken a heart of stone and made it receptive to His love and truth.

- He has promised sanctification in your life through Christ's power. A part of that is the wisdom to see your current situation and His word to show you your new identity and new beliefs.

- He has redeemed you from the bondage to old nature, rendering it powerless.

- He has shown you that your battle is now with the flesh. The old nature is rendered powerless to control you, but is a formidable bully. The power of Christ is stronger.

Will: *So what do I do from here?*

Matt: There is even more exciting news. You remember when the disciples pleaded with Christ after the resurrection to not leave them? Christ's response was that unless He left them the Father couldn't send the comforter…the Holy Spirit. God has not left you alone to fend for yourself. The Holy Spirit dwells in you and is the source of power and blessing in your daily life. Let me share more about this incredible investment into our lives. We cannot do it alone. We need His Spirit.

The Holy Spirit Seals the Deal!

Christ is in control and able to deliver hope for every aspect of our salvation… from spiritual birth to eternal glory. He is the author and perfecter of our faith (Hebrews 12: 2). The believer is redeemed (set free) from the domination and obligation of the old nature. However, even though we are not obligated to sin… our flesh (our old nature rendered powerless) is still in a corruptible state and apt to sin. (I John 1: 8-10). If this is the case, wouldn't we practically be obligated to sin since the very nature of the flesh is corrupted? We have clearly seen that the flesh (old nature) has no righteous quality in it. It is impossible to galvanize the flesh for any Godly intention.

The answer is yes. We would remain practically obligated to sin if the only act of sanctification was redeeming man from domination and obligation to sin. Despite this critical act, man would be technically free from the obligation to sin, but his heart (flesh nature) knows nothing but sin. The outcome, if salvation had only influenced man to this point, would leave him with only the flesh to pursue God. This would be futile. What sense would it make for Christ to redeem man from the obligation to the old nature and then leave it to man with only his natural unregenerate flesh to attempt to pursue righteousness? Many Christians instinctively picture themselves this way.

As mentioned earlier, some might say that the believer has a good dog (God) and a bad dog (sin) at work in them. Man finds himself between the two with a choice to make. The one that the believer feeds is the one that will be in control. This simple analogy leaves the good dog and bad dog equal in power. To put it another way…God is the "good dog" doing tricks and calisthenics to convince us of his love and dependability. The bad dog (Satan) competes to lure our attention away from the good dog with the enticements of this world in order to maintain control. In this illustration the decision is left to us to choose between the two. Our track record has already been proven. If left with only our own unregenerate self, the flesh will always choose what is self-advancing and self-gratifying. This is bad theology and would be awful for the believer if all God did was passively dwell as another voice and leave the bad dog loose. "That dog don't hunt"… practically or theologically speaking. It would leave man alone, still under the authority of the "old nature," to simply choose between two equal forces. God's work would have been incomplete and our lives would have been spiritually impotent. Fortunately, this is not the case. God did not leave the believer in a state of self-dependence. We were utterly dependent upon Christ for our initial salvation experience. We are equally dependent upon Him for every aspect of His sanctification process. God powerfully delivers.

Utilizing the two-dog analogy, let's look at a Biblical picture of what happened to the heart at salvation. Before we were saved, we (one dog, which was our own unregenerate state) were in control trying to work the world system to our advantage. We all created straw systems of beliefs and standards and set out to prove ourselves worthy, loved, unique and important. We were starving for fulfillment and seeking what was lost at the fall: intimacy, identity, and influence. We were dead to anything else and only knew our own means. Then, through His living word, Christ miraculously breathed life conversion. Through Christ, we were immediately placed in perfect standing with God through justification and reconciliation. Christ also redeemed us from the dominance of our old nature (bad dog), rendering it powerless. Our old nature no longer has ultimate authority and therefore, we are not obligated to sin. But if left in this state, we would have no choice but to sin because our being remains possessed only by our flesh (bad dog), not technically any longer in charge but practically our only alternative.

But something miraculous also happens at salvation. Through Christ, a new investment is made in man. We are endowed with a new heart and the Holy Spirit is invested in us.

Ezekiel 36:26-27

"I will give you a new heart and put a new spirit in you; I will remove from you your heart of stone and give you a heart of flesh. And I will put my spirit in you and move you to follow the decrees and be careful to keep my laws."

The new heart transformation endows the believer with the capacity for true spiritual consciousness, and the Holy Spirit provides crystal clear connection and empowerment among many other blessings from the One true God. Our very own being has been supernaturally changed. Something that wasn't there within us prior to salvation now dwells within us. It is the Holy Spirit that now resides in our new heart. Before, our old calloused heart of stone was dead to Christ. But now we have a whole new capacity, ability, and appetite to both know and seek the things of God. Christ's Spirit that dwells in our heart is actively moving the believer down the roadway of sanctification. All of this sounds so theological and technical, but it is really simply about God reaching out with unconditional love to redeem His children into a rich and rewarding relationship with Him.

This imparting of the Holy Spirit should not be confused with the "fillings" of the Spirit in the Old Testament (Psalm 51: 11; Isaiah 63: 11), even though there might still be "fillings" today. Those experiences were typically episodic by nature. Today, when a person comes into a relationship with Christ, a permanent indwelling of the Holy Spirit takes place (Romans 8: 9).

The Spirit that raised Jesus from the dead is the same Spirit that now dwells in the believer and gives "life." Before a person knows Christ, there is no good thing in him… no capacity for godliness at all (Romans 3: 9 – 18). But now the Spirit of Christ dwells within the believer's heart, imparting freedom… freedom from slavery, freedom to see, freedom from oppression, freedom to live for His glory. Isn't that what Christ's mission was! (Luke 4: 18 – 21)

Where there was only death, now there is life. The new believer is permanently filled with Christ's Spirit. The relationship is sealed. Not only are we to seek to abide in Him; he dwells in us. It is a constant connection with the lover of our soul. We are endowed with the presence of the Holy Spirit and all of the blessings of that relationship. Christ-centered supernatural transformation is at work within us.

The finishing touch to God's redemptive plan seals the deal.   At salvation a new heart and a new spirit, the Spirit of God, is invested into the new believer. This incredible endowment of God at salvation is a deposit guaranteeing what is to come.

II Corinthians 1:21-22

"Now it is God who makes both us and you stand firm in Christ. He anointed us, set His seal of ownership on us, and put His Spirit in our hearts as a deposit, guaranteeing what is to come."

II Corinthians 5: 17; Galatians 2: 20; Romans 8:9-11; II Corinthians 5:17; Ephesians 1:13-14; I Corinthians 3:16; II Corinthians 1:21-22

• The investment of the Holy Spirit is incredible. Please repeat out loud… yes I said out loud if you would… the following truths.

• The indwelling of His Spirit creates the privilege for constant companionship with Christ and abundant overflow.

- The Holy Spirit provides:
    - Constant attention
    - Love
    - Empowerment
    - Protection
    - Wisdom
    - Direction
    - Discipline to God's children

One can only imagine what the disciples must have felt as Christ was explaining that he would soon leave them to go back to the Father. Nothing short of fear and a sense of abandonment must have dominated their minds. They were learning utter dependence in Christ and now he was telling them that he was going to depart. John 14 shares Christ's assurance to His followers.

"[15]If you love me, you will obey what I command. [16]And I will ask the Father, and He will give you another Counselor to be with you forever– [17]the Spirit of truth. The world cannot accept Him, because it neither sees Him nor knows Him. But you know Him, for he lives with you and will be] in you. [18]I will not leave you as orphans; I will come to you. [19]Before long, the world will not see me anymore, but you will see me. Because I live, you also will live. [20]On that day you will realize that I am in my Father, and you are in me, and I am in you."

Jesus assured His followers that he would not make an orphan of them. In fact, it would be much the opposite. The promise of the Holy Spirit is the permanent connection with Christ. The Holy Spirit would indwell them permanently, providing constant companionship, comfort, and power. They were assured that they would never be out of Christ's sight, never distant to His wisdom and protective hand, and never away from His love and companionship.

In this passage the Holy Spirit is referred to as the Comforter. The Greek word for comforter is parakletos. This word literally means one who is called alongside to help. He further distinguishes the character of the helper. This helper is one exactly as He is (allos from the Greek). The one who had been "doing life" with them, loving them, guiding them, teaching them, comforting them, and sometimes disciplining them was promising He would be closer to them than their very own breath. The cross of Christ set us free. We are no longer in slavery. We are now under new ownership. We are indwelled by the Holy Spirit. The Holy Spirit indwells the believer to ignite within him a personalized, indescribable love and affection, empowerment of massive proportion, and guidance with wisdom and assurance.

Romans 8:9-11; I Corinthians 6:19-20; Ephesians 3: 20

"Now to Him who is able to do immeasurably more than all we ask or imagine, according to His power that is at work within us,"

Please read this paraphrase of Romans 8: 9 – 17.

Our old nature is dead (rendered powerless) and it no longer controls the believer. Our spirit is alive because of Christ's righteousness. Christ will give life to you moment by moment with the same power that raised Jesus from the dead. You no longer have any obligation to live according to the sinful nature. It only brings death. You now are empowered with the capacity to choose righteousness. Trust God's Spirit that indwells you and He will rid you of your sinful ways and bring real life and victory. This is because you are royalty, a true son of the living God, and have the blessings and inheritance that only a king's kid could wish for. Those old fears that once controlled your life are now senseless and impotent. You never need to be afraid again because your Abba Dad is in control and loves you and protects you. Always cry out for your Father… he likes it when you need him and he will never deny you. His Spirit will continually remind you that you are His. You will face ridicule, loss, and sometimes pain for Him, which is inevitable for His children. Always remember that it is for His glory which you will ultimately share in.

Think about it!

1. How does this section about the Holy Spirit affect your beliefs about your life journey?

2) For the redemption process to be complete, why was it vital for God to invest His Spirit into our lives?

3) Please list several ways the Holy Spirit operates in the believer's life.

4) How is the word "comforter" defined and why is that important to you?

5) Please read the following statement…

The Holy Spirit indwells the believer to ignite within him a personalized, indescribable love and affection, empowerment of massive proportion, and guidance with wisdom and assurance.

What stands out to you in this sentence and why?

Passage:

Ephesians 3:19-21

And to know this love surpasses knowledge—that you may be filled to the measure of all the fullness of God. Now to Him who is able to do immeasurably more than all we ask or imagine, according to His power that is at work within us, to Him be glory in the church and in Christ Jesus throughout all generations, for ever and ever! Amen.

Praise:

Worship the greatness and otherness of God who forms the universe by the work of his fingers (Ps 8).

Ponder:

Are there struggles or areas of your life that feel impossible? Talk to the God about the "immeasurably more than we can ask or imagine" about them.

Pray:

Father, all glory belongs to you. You are awesome in might and power. You are glorious! Fill me to the measure of all the fullness of You.

Chapter 10

Putting it all Together!

Meeting 5

Matt: How was your week?

Will: *This past week has been better.*

Matt: Good! In what way?

Will: *The section on the Holy Spirit really comforts me… no pun intended. There was so much about the Holy Spirit that was a mystery to me, and frankly still is. But to know that I am not alone at all and that God has invested the Holy Spirit in me guaranteeing what is to come…how cool is that. I continue to be amazed at how nothing was left to chance when God set us free. He had a plan, a complete and well thought-out plan.*

Matt: That will preach!

Will: *After we met last week I took Jenn to dinner and we had a great conversation. It took a little explaining, but she really connected with what we have been talking about. I feel more encouraged.*

Matt: That's great! I figured that she would understand.

Will: *I was talking with her a couple of nights ago and I realized that before last month I had all but given up.*

Matt: In what way?

Will: *I had lost hope in being any different. Looking back, I can even tell that my personal connection with God felt like it was fading. I guess I felt I was distant to God and moving backwards.*

Matt: Since then what has happened.

Will: *It hasn't been easy… I can tell you that. Facing the reality of my sinfulness and selfishness has been hard. I had no idea what I had hidden deep inside and all of my defense patterns. I knew that I got hurt, defensive, and controlling, but I never realized how much. I had no idea what was going on inside. I really was very seldom happy. The more I have thought about it the more I realize the incredible new hope I have in Christ. I sense that I am moving toward Christ and hope in Him and away from the slavery I have lived with for so long… the desperate need for approval. I built a major straw system to support my pride. I also realized that I treated others like they were my slaves.*

Matt: Those are big discoveries! When you think about it, those straw systems become idols that we constantly serve. And it takes some serious honesty and authenticity to walk into them. God has really been at work in you!

Will: *Hey, I met late last week with my two co-workers. They were a little quiet at the beginning of the meeting, but then I just put it out there. I first asked their forgiveness for being defensive and controlling. I then thanked them for caring enough about their jobs and our company to speak candidly in any area that needs development. They were so shocked they were speechless at first. The whole demeanor in our relationship immediately changed.*

Matt: Unbelievable!

Will: *I couldn't stop there. I shared with them a little about my past and my current struggles. One of them is a fellow Christian. I had no idea where the other associate stood spiritually. The believer immediately thanked me for sharing and then promised to pray for me. The other one said that he appreciated my candor and the conversation made him curious about Christ.*

Matt: Needless to say you must have felt incredible.

Will: *I felt relieved in a way and very encouraged. A few months ago I was like a balloon ready to pop. I am now experiencing genuine relaxation for the first time at work. It is a great feeling! Matt, I'm hogging the conversation.*

Matt: No! Please, keep going.

Will: *I sure don't fully get it all, but my picture of God and the sense of closeness and desire have changed. As I said, it was kind of like I was just bumping along frustrated and going to church because that's just what I know to do; but having almost no real interaction with God. The Bible seemed dry. In a way, I guess deep inside, I had gotten to a point where I really didn't see Christianity as practically helpful. I wouldn't admit I felt disappointed in God. We as believers just don't do that. Ultimately, I guessed that I was going to be stuck. Now there's a bunch of convoluted emotion... let me see you do something with that!*

The gospel not only clears the pathway for deep and abiding relationship with Christ, but it also impacts our relationships with all we are around. You can see in the dialogue with Will the great impact it has made internally and externally. Based upon the extensive promises of the cross below.

Promises from God's Word

John 1:12	I am God's child.
John 15:15	I am Christ's friend.
John 15:16	I will bear Christ's fruit.
Romans 5:1	I am completely forgiven and made righteous.
Romans 5: 1	I am fully pleasing to God.
Romans 5:1	I am free to live a life of righteousness.
Romans 6:1-6	I am dead to sin and it no longer rules my life.
Romans 8:1	I am free forever from condemnation.
Romans 8:14-15	I am God's dearly loved son.
Romans 8: 30	I have full assurance of eternal life.
I Corinthians 1:12	I can depend on God to sanctify me.
I Corinthians 2:16	I have been given the mind of Christ.
I Corinthians 3:16	I am God's temple.
II Corinthians 5:17	I am a new creation.
II Corinthians 5:18-19	I am reconciled to God.
Galatians 2:20	I no longer live, but Christ lives in me.
Galatians 4:6-7	I am an heir of God's blessing.
Ephesians 1:1	I am a saint.
Ephesians 1:3	I am blessed with every spiritual blessing.
Ephesians 2:10	I am God's handiwork.
Ephesians 3:12	I may approach God with confidence.
Colossians 1:22	I am totally loved and accepted by God.
Colossians 1:13	I am delivered from darkness.
Colossians 1:14	I have been forgiven of sin.
Colossians 2: 7	I am being built up in Christ.
Colossians 2:10	I have been made complete in Christ.
Colossians 3:12	I am chosen, holy, and dearly loved.
I Thessalonians 5:5	I am living in light and not in darkness.
II Timothy 1:7	I have the spirit of love, power, and self-control.
Hebrews 3:14	I share in Christ's life.
Hebrews 12:1	I have been created with purpose.
I Peter 2:9-10	I am a chosen race, royal priesthood, holy nation, and a people for God's possession.
I Peter 2:11	I am an alien and a stranger in this world.
II Peter 1:4	I am a partaker in God's nature.
I John 4: 9, 10	I am "at one" with God.
I John 5:18	I am born of God and the evil one can't touch me.

Instructions: Please pick out three promises from the preceding page and fill in the following chart.

1.
2.
3.

Impact from the promises of The Cross!

Christ-centered Attitude and Action

How do the promises of The Cross affect your attitude toward life?

Toward God

Toward Circumstances

Toward Yourself

Toward Others

Toward Your Past

Prayer Needs — What are the particular areas that need prayer based upon the prior answers?

Area Needing Faith	Scripture Passage	Promise

Steps of Faith: What are the particular steps of faith that need to be taken?

Toward	Steps of Faith
God	
Circumstances	
Yourself	
Others	
Your past	

Continuing Conversation…

Matt: What about moving forward?

Will: *As I said a few minutes ago, thank God for the investment of the Holy Spirit in our lives. But this is where I'm afraid. I have been through spiritual highs before. They went away as fast as they came. I am afraid that I will lose my fervor and find myself back where I was… maybe even more frustrated and cynical.*

Matt: Outside of the feelings, is there anything different this time?

Will: *I think so. I have a much greater understanding of the power of the cross. I understand better my attitudes and actions. I see my insecurity and where it was coming from. I feel like I am being very authentic and honest with myself, with others, and most importantly with God. I have been in performance mode for so long that it barricaded me off from seeing my struggles. It wasn't as though I had committed murder or something, but the absence of joy and peace in my life was a huge loss. As a result of this process I believe that I can truly approach God just the way I am. I know He loves me and welcomes me unconditionally.*

Matt: Man… I couldn't have summed it up that well. As you know, the graph indicating the pathway has grown throughout the chapters. Let's take a minute and look at the graph we have been building. I think that it will serve as a good reminder, and we can add a couple of things that will point you in the right direction.

✝ **Take the Gospel to Heart**

1. People Involved
2. Perceived Threat
3. Initial Feelings
4. Inward Reaction
5. Outward Disposition
6. Foundational Belief
7. Core Messages
8. ✝ The Cross of Christ
9. New Christ-Centered Beliefs
10. New Christ-Centered Attitude
11. New Christ-Centered Response
12. God Glorified Through Christ in You!

Will: *I had no idea that we were tackling all of that. If I had known what we were going to do in advance, it would have been overwhelming. But going one step at a time allowed me to understand and digest it.*

Matt: You can see how the dynamics have changed on the graph. Before you were caught in the spin of despair, but now you are rescued from the fleshly spin by Christ. He set you free to live in His truth and power. The result of identifying fleshly foundational beliefs and taking them to the cross is new Christ-centered beliefs, attitudes, and actions.

Will: *I am still a little afraid. You have no idea how deep this thing runs. As I said before the last thing I need is just another spiritual high. I know that I am experiencing new freedom based upon the cross, His word, and the Holy Spirit. But what do I do from my end?*

Matt: I can fully understand your concern. This is a big deal… but at the risk of sounding like I am throwing around a cliché… Our God is big enough to handle you. I know you now understand that you must depend upon Christ as much for your spiritual growth as you did for your salvation.

Will: *I want to make sure that I keep depending on Him and daily take the gospel to heart. I don't want to fall back into the old pattern.*

Matt: Let's talk about what has gotten you here to this point. You mentioned some of the major points a minute ago. But let's review in detail. It will help you understand how to make sure to move forward in victory. How would you describe where you began?

Will: *It all started with despair, what I now understand as the spin of despair. It was initially defeating. But as we looked at my situation Biblically, I realized that my despair was a result of my dependence upon my flesh. Even when I tried to use spiritual means it didn't seem to work. I realize now I was trying to do it in my own strength. That was just another form of fleshly effort. We identified specific fleshly beliefs that were holding me captive in my life.*

Matt: What happened then?

Will: *I came to a point of absolute defeat and felt there was no hope. I thought that defeat would be the worst thing that could happen, but now I realize it led me to a point that I have never been except when I originally accepted Christ… willing to cry out and declare my brokenness before God. I realized that I couldn't do it on my own. To grow spiritually I had to depend on Christ alone like I did when I got saved. I also realized that this is the position that God wants me… in a place that is utterly dependent upon Christ. God's word began giving me a lot of hope. I realized that through the cross I had a new heart that had a capacity for God's work in my life. We studied the word about how the cross redeemed me from the old nature and it was no longer a superpower in my life holding me captive. Even though it's still there, it*

	no longer dominates me. It's only a bully. That was very encouraging.
Matt:	You're not kidding!
Will:	*Then we looked at how God secured His incredible work by investing the Holy Spirit into our lives. We prayed out loud together and asked God to move in and set me free.*
Matt:	Unbelievable Will! Despair-Brokenness-Dependency. What has happened as a result?
Will:	*For the first time since accepting Christ years ago I feel like I am at peace… both with God and with myself. I sense greater freedom and joy. There is a real sense of closeness to God. Knowing more about His unconditional love and acceptance is beginning to change not only my thought processes but my relationships… like with my family and co-workers.*

Please take a minute and carefully review Will's Worksheet on the next page. On the following page fill in your own story.

Will's Worksheet

Take the Gospel to Heart

1. People Involved: Two Co-workers

2. Perceived Threat(s): Challenged my leadership / Said I didn't listen / Conversation digressed

3. Initial Feeling: Anger

4. Inward Reaction: Blame later turning to shame

5. Outward Disposition: Controlling/ Withdrew/ Wouldn't Listen

6. Foundational Beliefs

I feel I am _successful_ when _I am fully competent and others know it_.

I feel that I am _significant_ when _things go as I plan it and no one questions me_.

7. Core Messages

From	Message	Feeling Response
1 Educators/ friends/ family	You are not competent/ you are not bright/ you never finish anything well/ you're going to fail in life	Embarrassment Shame Fear
2		

8. ✝ The Cross

The Promise	New Belief **9**	New Attitude **10**
1 Reconciled	I am secure in the fact that I am unconditionally loved and accepted by God	I am free from fear of rejection. Feel secure in Him. My success is founded in Christ's work.
2 Sanctified, Adopted, Created with Purpose	I am hopeful because God is sanctifying me, loves me as a son, has a planned purpose	Feel excited and hopeful. Can see God greatly at work in me. Failures are opportunities to grow. I don't need to compete or try to be something I am not.

11. Response to People: Ablwe to share authentically, be myself, remain teachable, teach others out of weakenss, share my faith

12. Response to God: Christ Glorified through... my trust and faith in Him, my delighting in Him, my ministry of weakness to others

Please fill out your own Take the Gospel to Heart Worksheet.

Take the Gospel to Heart

1 People Involved _____

2 Perceived Threat(s) _____

3 Initial Feeling _____

4 Inward Reaction _____

5 Outward Disposition _____

6 Foundational Beliefs

I feel I am _____ when _____.

I feel that I am _____ when _____.

7 Core Messages

From	Message	Feeling Response
1		
2		

8 ✝ The Cross

The Promise	New Belief **9**	New Attitude **10**
1		
2		

11 Response to People

12 Response to God

Chapter 11

Intimacy...The Spiritual Fuel for the Heart

Meeting 5 continues

Will: *Wow Matt, things continue to progress. It feels weird to have the awareness of sin without going into the doldrums and to know that Christ is using this conviction in order to point me toward dependence in Him.*

Matt: Biblically and practically speaking, this is about taking every thought captive for Christ. I Corinthians 10:5 states... "We demolish arguments and every pretension that sets itself up against the knowledge of God, and we take every thought to make it obedient to Christ". The process we've been through simply served to help you identify fleshly thinking, know how to take those thoughts captive by filtering them through God's word, and trusting Christ for your new identity in Him.

Will: *But I am still curious about my part, my responsibility.*

Matt: So the question is what is your responsibility to make sure this dependency keeps on happening. Remember what I shared with regard to sanctification. Let me remind you...

"So what do I do? Cling to Christ. Depend upon Him. Remember you are broken and needy. Sanctification is the process of realizing our insufficiency and Christ's sufficiency. We are responsible to remain in a state of brokenness and dependency upon Him. Even that is dependent upon

Him. If you sense you have taken over, which we often do, invite Christ to bring you back to that place of need. Progressive sanctification is indeed a process. The believer's faith is in perpetual motion moving between Christ (brokenness, dependency, clinging to Christ) and self (pride, independence, clinging to the world). But God is faithful even when we are not. With His love and discipline, he continues to compel us throughout the sanctification process, bringing us closer to dependence in Him alone (II Cor. 5: 14; Hebrew 12: 6). Just like my hope for salvation, my hope for sanctification is in Christ alone. Except for His great work, I realized I was completely helpless. What seemed like defeat for me simply led me back to where I began when I received Christ… dependent upon Him."

Progressive sanctification is a process. There will be days where you are very dependent upon Christ and there will be times when you stray. The difference this time is you now know the pathway to victory.

Will: *It's getting clearer.*

Matt: Well, let's talk about what it's not…it's not about hopelessness; it's not about personal shame or blaming others; it's not trying to spiritually pull yourself up by your own bootstraps; it's not about chasing a fleshly fix to sedate your pain or go into some kind of denial. These are all part of the straw systems of the flesh… our idols. Remember that stuff?

Will: *Boy, do I ever!*

Matt: It is about remaining in a state of awareness that neediness creates dependency in Christ. It is about identifying wrongful beliefs and rather than moving to blame, shame, denial or medicate the pain, take them to the cross. Take them to Christ and confess these fleshly beliefs for what they are… sin. Invite Him to show the truth in His word. Invite Him to take control. You need to trust that God is in on this "big time." I want to encourage you to hold his hand, so to speak, but know that he will never let go of your hand. He is actively pursuing you. It's not only Biblically true, but in your case it is experientially obvious.

Will: *That is encouraging because I don't trust myself.*

Matt: That's the point! I don't trust myself either, but we do trust Christ. Relationship is the key. There are a couple of incredible blessings that we haven't yet talked about that are our means to incredible intimacy with God. They are our sustenance, our food for vitality and consistency. They keep us centered. It is vital that we understand the full extent of them.

Will: *What are you referring to?*

Matt: I am talking about the supernatural power of His word and prayer.

Will: *Don't most Christians know this?*

Matt: Well, let me ask you? What is your first response when I mention Bible study and prayer? Is it an immediate sense of elation with the privilege to encounter Christ and experience His presence? Does it enthrall you to know that every morsel of His living word will supernaturally transform your heart outlook, and actions for His glory? Does it thrill you to know that you may enter into that most Holy place and have our great God's interest and attention? Do you highly anticipate an intimate gathering where He pours His love, hope, and peace upon you?

Will: *Do you?*

Matt: Not often enough, but more and more. What I do know is Christ has broken down the barrier, re-engaged full access to intimate relationship, and invited us to come and consume. How cool is that!

Will: *The truth is when I initially hear Bible study and prayer, it conjures up feelings like… old news, of course, a good habit, time constraints… and unfortunately, if I'm really honest, guilt and mundane. It certainly doesn't create a feeling like I might have going to a playoff game or what I felt when Jenn and I first started dating. I certainly don't anticipate a divine encounter with God.*

Matt: You're reading my mind. Couldn't agree more. It's almost like we're inoculated with an inability to truly get this. But let's face it, our flesh isn't attracted to this encounter and the evil one himself will do anything possible to tempt us away from these encounters with God.

The Means to Intimacy… His Word and Prayer

The challenge the believer faces is to abide in a relationship with Christ. Calvin says it this way…

"Moreover, he sets the corruption of the world in opposition to the divine nature; but he shows that this corruption is not in the elements which surround us, but in our heart, because there vicious and depraved affections prevail, the fountain and root of which he points out by the word lust." The strength of the believer is found in an abiding relationship with Christ. Therefore, the primary goal in battling the flesh is to execute God's Biblical plan that promotes intimacy and dependence upon Christ. II Peter 1: 1 – 4 clearly teaches us this."

The heart is the vital organ of the believer. The heart is the center of man… his being. His consciousness, intelligence, moral fabric, seat of emotions, personality, beliefs, and his will reside in the heart. Another way to describe the heart is man's inner self. Before salvation, he is dead in sin and his heart is hopelessly wicked. Through Christ at salvation, the believer's heart is supernaturally transformed. I don't pretend to be able to explain the mystery of how God does this; but this I do know, a heart that was once completely spiritually dead now has life… a new life in Christ. The new heart now has a tender spiritual capability enabling the believer to experience Christ-given faith, hope, and enlightenment and to willfully trust the power of the Holy Spirit for obedience and spiritual fruit. The old nature remains, but is dethroned (rendered powerless), and now the flesh (old nature rendered powerless) has no authority, but acts as a bully and will try to remain in control.

1. When scripture speaks of the heart, what is it referring to?

2. What was the spiritual heart of man like before salvation?

3. How is the new heart different?

4. What was the old nature like before salvation?

5. Who is it different after salvation?

6. Why is a discussion on the heart important to our spiritual victory?

The new heart transformation endows the believer with the capacity for true spiritual consciousness. The Holy Spirit provides crystal clear connection and empowerment with God. The believer's being has been supernaturally changed. The Holy Spirit resides in the new heart giving the believer a whole new hunger, pathway, and ability to both know and seek the things of God. Christ's Spirit is actively moving the believer down the roadway of sanctification. His Spirit supernaturally comforts, teaches, speaks to our heart, gives direction, bears spiritual fruit, gives and empowers spiritual gifts, brings human prayers before the throne room of God, assures the believer of His adoption, and brings glory to God.

II Peter 1: 3, 4

"³His divine power has given us everything we need for life and godliness through our knowledge of Him who called us by His own glory and goodness. ⁴Through these He has given us His very great and precious promises, so that through them you may participate in the divine nature and escape the corruption in the world caused by evil desires."

1. II Peter 1: 3, What do you think God means when he promises life and godliness?

2. He shares in the same passage that life and godliness is a result of our knowledge of him. What do you think that means?

3. Where does this knowledge come from? (vs. 4)

4. What do you think it means to "participate in the divine nature?"

II Peter 1: 3, 4 teaches that the believer is given everything necessary for life and godliness. The believer has been given "great and precious promises" so that he may literally "participate in the divine nature and escape the corruption of the world caused by evil desires." How cool is that! The believer is promised the privilege of participating in the divine nature and enjoying the fruit of life and godliness. The passage also clearly teaches that the key to participating in the divine nature and living in victory over the flesh is one of knowledge, specifically "knowledge of Him."

1. When you read the words "knowledge of Him," what first comes to your mind?

Typically, when Christians think of "knowledge" they tend to think of an accumulation of accurate information about a subject. Certainly accuracy is important when it comes to knowledge, but in this passage it means so much more.

Epignosis, the Greek word for knowledge in this passage, means "true knowledge" or "exact, complete, thorough, accurate, experiential knowledge. Not just abstract, intellectual, head knowledge of God or even facts about Him."[1] In other words, these promises and this victory are appropriated within the context of relationship… not just any relationship, but an intimate relationship with Christ Jesus who is the true deliverer. This key to victory, relational intimacy and the overflow of that relationship, underscores the original purpose of creation and the following redemption of man through Christ, intimate relational connection for His glory! It was the loss of this "knowledge" (intimate connection with God) resulting from the fall that brought death. It is the restoration of this relationship through Christ that provides the overflow of divine victory. If the believer is vitally connected to the vine (Christ) he will bear the vine's fruit (Jn. 15). It is out of this relational intimacy that the believer overflows with the power to participate in God's divine nature and escape the corruption of the world. The emphasis should be placed on the source of the fruit rather than the fruit itself, as important as it is. This passage is not a command, but a promise of overflow as a result of our divine connection to Christ.

1. How does understanding of the Greek word "Epignosis" affect the way you view your relationship with God?

John Piper says this about II Peter 2: 2…

"But probably the most important thing to notice in verse 2 is that God's grace and peace are multiplied in or through the knowledge of God. Peter cannot get past his second sentence without exposing one of his deepest convictions: namely, that knowing God is the means by which his grace and peace become large and powerful in our lives. If you want to enjoy God's peace and be the aroma of his grace in the world, your knowledge of him has to grow. Grace is not a mere deposit. It is a power that leads to godliness and eternal life. And where knowledge of the glory and excellence of God languishes, grace does not flow. The channel from God's infinite reservoir of grace into and through our lives is knowledge of God. We do not study the Scripture for its own sake, but because through it comes the knowledge of God, and through that grace and peace are multiplied in your heart in the church and in the world. In the next two verses of our text Peter builds on this connection now between knowledge of God and the power of grace." [1] II Peter 1 (Precept Austin)

The purpose of Christ's work was to redeem man and restore his relationship with God. Victory is the overflow of that intimacy. Therefore, ongoing relational intimacy with Christ is the key to victory. It is within this relational intimacy with Christ that the believer finds his source of true love, power, and fulfillment. The vital conduit for this relational connection is God's word and prayer.

This vital connection providing necessary intimacy is so misunderstood and grossly underestimated. Often, the minute God's word (Bible) is mentioned, there are immediate mental responses within people. It is easy for some to think of His word as another piece of ancient literature to glean wisdom. Or a precious book (which it is) handed down from generation to generation (which it was) that by nature of its age we ascribe respectful and sentimental value. Oops… wrong. This isn't an issue of mere respect and sentiment. Among believers, they may "check out" having been inoculated by over-familiarity with little true understanding. And still others have made it an object of discipline versus a conduit of relationship, missing the whole heart of the blessing. Please listen carefully.

The truth is God's word and prayer are the extraordinarily supernatural, life-giving means and primary pathways to commune with God. His word is a primary means of relationship where He displays His love and deploys His heart-changing provision and power to man's heart. Prayer is the vital conduit by which the believer responds to His glory through praise, confession, thanksgiving, to seek wisdom, enjoy community, pouring out one's heart, listening, and requesting. This circle of communication mutually fulfills both God and man giving both what they most desire… intimacy with one another! God delights in this intimacy and man lives in the glorious shadow of His delight.

Let's take a brief look at His word.

It is a mystery as to how His word supernaturally impacts the hearts of those he intends. I Peter 1: 23 says…"For you have been born again, not of perishable seed, but of imperishable, through the living and enduring word of God." God's word is living. It has always been living. It is supernaturally breathing and active.

Please look up the following passages and fill in the blanks.

It is His word that spoke _____ (Gen. 1).

It was God's word that _____ (Gen. 15).

His words _____ (Exodus 14: 21)

Christ is the _____ that became flesh (Jn. 1: 1).

It is His word _____ (Jn. 4:46 -53).

It is His word that _____ (Matt. 8:28 – 33).

It is His word that _____ (Luke 7:12 – 16).

His word is _____ (Ps. 18:30).

His word is _____ (Ps. 56: 10).

His word is _____ (Ps. 119: 160)

His word _____ (Isa. 40: 8).

His word _____ to those who obey it (Luke 11: 28).

His word is _____ (Jn. 3: 34).

His word is _____ …our very sustenance (Matt. 4: 4).

His word _____ (Jn. 17: 17).

Cheat sheet

Gen 1… the universe into existence

Gen. 15… gave visions to prophets

Ex. 14: 21… part seas and control the winds

Jn. 1: 1… Word

Jn. 4: 46 – 53… that heals

Matt. 8: 28 – 33… makes demons run

Luke 7: 12 - 16… raises the dead

Ps. 18: 30… flawless

Ps. 56: 10… praiseworthy

Ps. 119: 160… true

Isa. 40: 8… stands forever

Luke 18: 28… brings blessing

Jn. 3: 34… spoken by the Holy Spirit

Matt. 4: 4… our food

Jn. 17: 17… sanctifies the believer

To deepen this understanding of His word, please take a moment and read the passage below aloud as you dwell on the incredible riches our great God shares about His word. Following the passage, please fill out the meditation guide.

How beautiful is this picture of His word found in Ps. 19!

[7] The law of the LORD is perfect,
reviving the soul.
The statutes of the LORD are trustworthy,
making wise the simple.

[8] The precepts of the LORD are right,
giving joy to the heart.
The commands of the LORD are radiant,
giving light to the eyes.

[9] The fear of the LORD is pure,
enduring forever.
The ordinances of the LORD are sure
and altogether righteous.

[10] They are more precious than gold,
than much pure gold;
they are sweeter than honey,
than honey from the comb.

[11] By them is your servant warned;
in keeping them there is great reward.

Meditation Exercise:

My initial thoughts from the passage were…

As I dwelled on the passage God showed me…

God's works and ways and purposes and promises that became clearer to me were…

Applying the passage to myself (how I currently view life and act) led me to see…

In light of meditation of this truth, I pray that I might…

What we're talking about is truth that, when empowered by the Holy Spirit and applied to the fertile heart of a believer, creates a supernatural life-giving effect transforming the very heart of that person (Jn. 6: 63). It gives life! Let me say it again… it gives life!

His word imparts love.

His word imparts truth.

His word imparts comfort.

His word imparts direction.

His word imparts hope.

His word imparts power.

His word imparts discipline.

His word imparts identity.

His word makes promises.

His word protects.

His word gives life.

Hebrews 4:12

"For the word of God is living and active. Sharper than any double-edged sword, it penetrates even to dividing soul and spirit, joints and marrow; it judges the thoughts and attitudes of the heart."

As said before, His word is living and active. It is able to penetrate at the deepest levels shining light into the heart, uncovering the confusions, and unraveling the conflicts in order to root out what is of the flesh. It then breathes life-giving truth, hope, and power found in dependence upon Christ (I Thess. 2: 13). His word is able to take the believer's heart, which was once defiled, and consecrate (set apart for sacred purposes) it for His glory. His word is nothing short of a miraculous supernaturally charged arsenal used by the Holy Spirit to breathe eternal life into His children (I Timothy 4: 5). His word initiated life in the believer and keeps on giving life! His word is God-breathed and makes the believer wise and fully equipped for salvation. Listen to how Paul addresses Timothy with regard to God's word.

II Timothy 3

"[15] and how from infancy you have known the holy Scriptures, which are able to make you wise for salvation through faith in Christ Jesus. [16] All Scripture is God-breathed and is useful for teaching, rebuking, correcting and training in righteousness, [17] so that the man of God may be thoroughly equipped for every good work."

Therefore, stand under the cleansing, refreshing, and life-giving waters of God's precious word. Seek after it like a thirsty deer pants after water (Ps. 42: 1).

Let the word of Christ dwell in you richly (Colossians 3: 16).

Let His word light up your pathway (Ps. 119: 104).

Let His truth purify your heart (Acts 15: 9).

Experience His inexpressible love (Eph. 3: 18 – 19).

Let it engage you with His unlimited blessings (Luke 1: 37).

Let it uproot the old distortions and perversions that once dominated your life and impart the truth and power of freedom. (Hebrews 4:11-13).

Let it expose and demolish strongholds.

Let it take captive every thought for Christ (II Cor. 10: 3 – 6).

Let it nourish your soul (Matt. 4: 4).

Let it run rampant in your heart splashing out on others (Luke 6:45).

Let it set you free (Jn. 8: 31, 32).

Hide His word in your heart (Ps. 119: 11).

Proverbs 2: 1 – 6

¹My son, if you accept my words
and store up my commands within you,

²turning your ear to wisdom
and applying your heart to understanding,

³and if you call out for insight
and cry aloud for understanding,

⁴and if you look for it as for silver
and search for it as for hidden treasure,

⁵then you will understand the fear of the LORD
and find the knowledge of God.

⁶For the LORD gives wisdom,
and from his mouth come knowledge and understanding.

What more can be said about the supernatural power of God's word. That is like drinking from a fire hydrant. So much it overwhelms… but good stuff!

1) What surprised you about what you read about His word?

2. Please read Hebrews 4:12.
"For the word of God is living and active. Sharper than any double-edged sword, it penetrates even to dividing soul and spirit, joints and marrow; it judges the thoughts and attitudes of the heart."

What is God saying in this passage?

Why do you think it is important?

3) The author said these words…

His word is nothing short of a miraculous supernaturally charged arsenal used by the Holy Spirit to breathe eternal life into His children (I Timothy 4: 5).

Do you often think of His word like this?   Yes   No

If you did more often, how would it affect your time in His word?

Passage:

Psalm 116:5

The Lord is gracious and righteous; our God is full of compassion.

Romans 5:17

For if, by the trespass of the one man, death reigned through that one man, how much more will those who receive God's abundant provision of grace and of the gift of righteousness reign in the life through the one man, Jesus Christ!

Praise:

Worship the Lord who is gracious, righteous, and full of compassion. Thank him for giving you the gift of righteousness.

Ponder:

Listen to the Father wooing you to great victory. Hear him asking you what the "much more of living in righteousness and reigning through Jesus Christ" looks like for you.

Pray:

Jesus, your abundant and amazing grace and your precious gift of righteousness gives me the joy of experiencing victory in life. Guide me day by day into more of this victorious life you have provided.

Chapter 12

It's even Better!

Let's take a look at Prayer.

It's beyond human comprehension to think that we, God's children, have constant privilege and access into the throne room of Jehovah God. When I think about this, I am reminded of the picture we see in Exodus 33 regarding Joshua. When Moses would make his way into the tent of meeting with God, scripture shares that Joshua would stake out a position as close to the tent as possible and would remain long after Moses exited the tent. Joshua yearned for the opportunity to meet with God as Moses did... and God certainly did not deprive him of this desire.

Today, as a result of the work of Christ, the believer has complete access into that innermost place to abide with his Abba Father. Hebrews 4: 16 says… "Let us then approach God's throne of grace with confidence, so that we may receive mercy and find grace to help us in our time of need." We know that Paul had a habit of regular prayer. However, he shared a desire to remain in a constant state of prayer experiencing Christ's presence. (I Thessalonians 5: 17)

I will never forget in 1979 when I was given the opportunity to meet Ronald Reagan. He was a human hero to me. Meeting him created incredible anticipation and then a wonderful few moments of unforgettable dialogue. I am sure you have your stories of a touch with fame.

If we could understand the full significance of the privilege of intimacy with God and the resulting power, I am sure we would not only rush to prayer, but like Paul, crave never leaving His presence. If you are like I am, this particular privilege is often neglected. I find myself too busy, wondering if I am really heard, questioning the value, my mind wandering, or even completely distracted. Sometimes I fall asleep. Another deterrent comes with poor understanding of our rights as His children and feeling shut out due to the misunderstanding. We feel we need to have everything together to approach God rather than to come just the way we are. The truth is we don't get right to get to God, but getting to God gets us right! Only through Christ are we given the privilege of prayer. One other thing is for sure… like his hatred for God's word, the evil one wants to cut us off from this incredible relational connection. He has no ability to interrupt the supernatural hand of God in or through our prayer life once we enter in. So he'll do anything to keep us out.

Think about it!

1. Have you experienced a "touch with fame?" If so, who was it and what was your response?

2) Joshua desperately desired to meet with God. At the cross, all barriers were torn and believers are invited to enter into His throne room. (Hebrews 4: 16) What should this incredible opportunity mean to the believer?

3) Which of the distractions that the author mentioned can you identify with? Do you have others?

4) How would your actions define your current perspective of prayer?

What happens when we pray?

As we meet with Him we find a safe place. We bask under His love. We share our praise and adoration for Him. We confess our sin. We shower Him with thanksgiving. We sometimes moan and grunt. We enjoy His community. We invite Him to speak to us. We listen. We invite Him to transform our heart. We make requests on our own behalf. We seek His heart and then make intercession in behalf of others. Our mighty God then releases lightning bolts of blessings.

The following paraphrase comes directly from God's word. The supporting passages are found beneath each paragraph.

An Invitation to you…

Come in. I want to be with you. I adore you. Come into my throne room with confidence. Come as you are. No, ignore the devil as he wishes a ransom, one that is too pricey for you to pay… and unnecessary… I paid it. My son Jesus has redeemed you and made you perfect in our sight. I continue to sanctify you. You owe nothing. Don't wait. I have invested my Spirit in you. He will help you in my throne room. Oh, by the way, Jesus always talks with me about you! You feel like you don't know what to say? Don't be bashful. Just share from your heart. Cry out to me. My Spirit will intercede in your behalf. Enter boldly. No, don't stop there. Come all the way in to the Most Holy Place. The blood of my son gives you that liberty. A little closer if you will. You can be fully confident. Through my son you are clean and washed with my pure water. Don't have the least bit of fear. I understand your challenges and temptations. I have been there. I delight in making your steps firm. I am in control. I will be faithful to you. I love you!

Hebrews 4: 14 – 16; Jn. 10: 10; Heb. 10: 12 – 16; Rom. 8: 26, 27; Ps. 37: 23; Heb. 4: 14 – 16

My child! Yes… you heard me. You are indeed my child. You are the King's kid. Not just any King's kid… but the King of King's kid. You are an heir. You are my beloved! I dance over you! I delight in you! I rejoice over you with singing! Please relax in my love. I will never leave you or forsake you. I delight in taking care of you! Oh, you ask… how is this possible? It is because of Christ Jesus!

Gal. 4: 3 – 7; Deut. 33: 12; Zephaniah 3: 17; Hebrews 13: 5; Ps. 51; 17

I, the Mighty King, the Creator, The Holy One, the Lord of Lords, The Alpha and Omega, Your Savior---- I, the one who forms the mountains, creates the wind, reveals his thoughts to man, who turns the dawn to darkness, and trends the high places of the earth--- the Lord God Almighty… I invite you to seek me and know me. My sons and daughters… co-heirs with Christ… come now! I see you and I am attentive to you.

Amos 4: 13; Rom. 8: 17; I Peter 3: 12

Ask… it will be given; seek and you shall find; knock and the door will be opened. Remain in me and trust my word and ask whatever you wish, and I will give it to you. It is for my glory that I do this. I want you to bear my abundant fruit. Ask in Jesus' name. You haven't asked enough. Ask and you will receive. I will make you complete. I will bless you with joy!

Matthew 7: 7 – 11; John 15: 7; John 16: 23 – 24

So you wish for a bit of help. Here it is. Rejoice in me! Praise my Holy Name! Give thanks to Him! Confess your sins to me. Don't let a list build up. I will forgive you and will cleanse you. I Jn. 1: 9

 Think about it!

1. What were your overall feelings about the paraphrased invitation?

2. In the invitation, which points in particular stood out?

For some the idea of prayer comes very easy. For others it can seem a bit discomforting and even embarrassing at first. For all believers, God's word gives a broad and incredible picture of how to pray.

Pray for direction.

Pray for strength over temptation.

Pray by faith knowing that you will receive.

Pray humbly and alone.

Make the church a house of prayer.

Pray often and in quiet places.

Devote yourself to prayer with others.

Pray for safety.

Pray that the Spirit will give wisdom and revelation.

Pray that you may be enlightened with the hope, riches, and power you have received.

Pray for His power to strengthen your inner being.

Pray that you may be rooted and established in His love.

Pray for knowledge, depth, and insight.

Pray for peace from anxiety.

Pray for others, for the knowledge of God's will, that they will with have wisdom and understanding.

Pray constantly to live worthy of His calling.

Pray when lacking in faith.

Pray in all circumstances with joy.

Pray that He will open the door for you to proclaim Christ.

Devote yourself to prayer.

Pray that you may please Christ in every way.

Pray that you will bear fruit.

Pray that you will grow in knowledge.

Pray if you are in trouble.

Pray by confessing your sins to one another.

Pray for other believers that they would be set free from sin.

I Chr. 16: 31; Deut. 32: 3; Ps. 28: 7; Jeremiah 42:3; Mark 14:38; Mark 11:24; Matthew 21:22; Matthew 6:6; Luke 19:46; Luke 5:16; Acts 2:42; Acts 27:29; Ephesians 1:17-19; Philippians 1:9; Philippians 4:6; Colossians 1:9; 2 Thessalonians 1:11; 1 Thessalonians 3:10; I Thessalonians 5: 17, 18; Colossians 4:3; Colossians 4:2; Colossians 1:10; James 5:13; James 5:16; 1 John 5:16.

Summary

Amazing! We enter His throne room as sons and daughters. We are warriors for the King of Kings. We are no different than Moses, David, Nehemiah, Ruth, Isaiah, Peter, or Paul… just different people living in a different era… but serving the same God who displays His love and power as he unveils His miraculous redemptive plan. History is unfolding as we speak… and we are a chosen part of His redeeming work. We have the ear of our great God. We are participants in His mighty redeeming work. We are invited to commune… to draw near unto Him. We are invited to seek. We are invited to ask. We, as the children of God, hold in our hands the honor to prompt God to move for His glory. Our God acts on these requests showering down lightning bolts of blessings. Can one estimate the privilege of prayer? Go! Go Now! Enjoy! Experience Him. Know that your Abba Father awaits your visit.

Meeting 6 (concluding meeting for Will and Matt)

(After a long enjoyable lunch together... that Will paid for!)

Will: *Over the last few months I feel like I have been drinking from a fire hose... particularly that last study on God's word and prayer.*

Matt: I know exactly how you feel. Regarding God's word and prayer... what were a few things you learned... or re-learned?

Will: *Well, first of all it was convicting. That was good. I first felt guilty but quickly recognized that was fleshly stuff and asked God to teach me. Once past that, I guess the best way to sum it up is how much Christ wants to "do life" with me. How incredible is it that Christ wants to be truly a friend... respectfully speaking. He wants to spend time with me, talk with me, me with Him... and in this case, mentor me. Pour His life into me.*

Matt: Whew! Couldn't say it better myself.

Will: *Everything else in the time together has been so helpful but I am afraid I am forgetting more than I am learning.*

Matt: I can understand what you mean. Have we been moving too fast?

Will: *Well, as I think about it, everything we talked about was important to understand. From the information perspective it's like putting a puzzle together... or better still... building a structure from the foundation up. But all of it points to the same conclusion.*

Matt: I would love to hear what you think that conclusion is.

Will: *Everything points back to Christ and the work of the cross... I guess I should say His continued work in my life as a result of the cross.*

Matt: Definitely... Lord, may we believe that more and more!

Will: *This past week I had several experiences where Christ gave me strength to pre-empt several challenges. Rather than fall victim like I normally would to my fleshly reaction, I caught myself getting ready to begin riding the spin of despair.*

Matt: Would you share an example?

Will: *Evening before last is a great example. I have been very busy so Jenn (wife) has been planning our vacation. I, of course, have been reminding her for a number of weeks that the summer is approaching fast and we need to get our plans made. She has assured me she is on it. Well, night before last, I overheard her on the phone trying to get our lodging settled. That is something that should have been done six weeks ago. See, listen to my controlling attitude! I immediately realized that I was very irritated and began to take the gospel to heart. I literally found myself asking myself why I felt*

	so intense… what are my inward feelings… what will my outward demeanor be if I don't take the gospel to heart? And then it happened… I simply quietly prayed and invited Christ into the situation. I confessed my fleshly anger and my controlling attitude even though I had not yet shown them. In Christ I don't need to fall victim to my fleshly beliefs and attitudes.
Matt:	Now that's a story that brings God glory! Wait a minute… how did it end?
Will:	*When I prayed I became immediately aware of that ugly side of me… my flesh. I asked Christ to forgive me of my attitude and asked for His Spirit to reign. The opposite of my fleshly frustration is gentleness and a servant's heart. I literally quoted Galatians 5: 22 and 23 to myself as a promise that I have received through Christ.*
Matt:	Now that is incredible! Taking every thought captive for Christ.
Will:	*Jenn was still in the kitchen so I went in. She looked miserable. She, of course, did not know that I knew what was going on. I went over to her and asked her why she looked so gloomy. Understandably, she hesitantly shared that she had ruined our vacation because of her procrastination. I could see her face wincing as she shared. She was afraid of me. I hurt for her. I have been such a bully.* (tears well up in Will's eyes)
Matt:	That's painful.
Will:	*I put my arms around her and held her. I know she must have been shocked. Then we went into the den and sat down and assured her that it would work out and that maybe the delay would even give us a better "last minute" deal. She began to relax. I know she was amazed. I then asked forgiveness for ever bullying her.*
Matt:	Will, God is so at work in you. I am so thankful you have bravely walked down this pathway.
Will:	*She just starred right at me a minute and then said... "do I know you?" The next evening we worked together and tracked down a great place at the beach. Honestly opening up and understanding my fleshly tendencies, growing in my understanding the power of the cross, and knowing how to seize the power of the cross from a position of brokenness and dependence really works. It is affecting every facet of my life from the little stuff to the big stuff. I feel freedom, closeness to Christ, and genuine spiritual growth like I have never felt before. To be honest, I wish that others could have peaked over our shoulder as we walked through the last few months.*
Matt:	Maybe we just did! Will, what a pleasure to journey with a friend like you! You are serving to teach me and remind me of many things that I easily forget. Thanks Friend!
Will:	*Thank you! See you soon.*

Please take a minute and journal your personal experience with this journey.

Think about it!

1. When you first began this journey, what were you expecting?

2. What are the main "take-aways" that you wish to remember?

3. How do you pray these will impact your life into your future?

4. What specific steps do you want to take in order to move forward in your relationship with Christ?

5. What do you want to say to Christ?

Passage:

John 15:3-5

You are already clean because of the word I have spoken to you. Remain in me, as I also remain in you. No branch can bear fruit by itself; it must remain in the vine. Neither can you bear fruit unless you remain in me. "I am the vine; you are the branches. If you remain in me and I in you, you will bear much fruit; apart from me you can do nothing.

Praise:

Jesus, you are the True Vine. Thank you for the unspeakable privilege of being able to remain in you.

Ponder:

Ask God where the areas are that you are trying to do life on your own apart from the Vine.

Pray:

Father, thank you that I am already clean because of the word Jesus has spoken. It is so easy to try to do things on my own. Thank you for your constant wooing of my heart back to you. Cause me to be grafted deeper into the True Vine. I long to remain in you in every moment of my day.

Appendix 1

Whatever Happened to Ginny and Cory?

I pray that this journey has helped you to identify fleshly patterns, define fleshly foundational beliefs, take them to the cross, and begin to experience Christ-empowered intimacy yielding freedom and victory. But you must wonder whatever happened to Ginny and Cory.

It is now your turn. I am not going to guide you through this. In the appendix I have shared the broad picture of Ginny and Cory's story line. Following each story I provide the same worksheets that you utilized throughout the study. I challenge you to read each of their stories and before looking at their outcomes in their worksheets, think through how you might approach their needs, and speak into it. I believe this process will further your understanding of your own journey as well as provide better understanding on how to walk someone else through the journey... to greater intimacy with Christ!

Instructions…

Please read the case studies and answer the clarifying questions as you go.

Case Study 1

Ginny

Age: 34

Family Status: Married for 12 years/ two children ages 9 and 5

Work Status: Primarily stay-at-home mom but with part-time job

Other: Christian since age 16. Actively using gifts of mercy and teaching in church and community.

Episode:

Ginny fell to the floor in tears, angry and frustrated. What had seemingly been a minor disagreement with her husband escalated into an angry fit. Her loving family stood helplessly in the wake of this painful outburst. About once a month she would cascade into emotional distress, plunging into angry outbursts that eventually led to a high sense of shame. It seemed to Ginny that others were to be blamed… like they were purposely provoking her. She hated these episodes but couldn't seem to do anything about them. How could she escape this spin of despair? Her normally quiet and loving temperament would plunge into the pits of anger.

Ginny's fleshly logic was… "I perceive my husband as directive or condescending whenever he disagrees with me. That makes me feel reactive anger resulting from feeling devalued and disrespected. After careful discussion with Ginny she realized that she was highly reactive to any input, suggestion, or push back from her husband. This felt directive to her. When he would react to her anger, she felt that any defense was condescending. Things would normalize after several days until the next eruption.

After initially blaming others, Ginny realized that there was something deeper inside that kept her "on edge." Ginny sought help to try to better understand her spin of despair.

 Think about it!

Based upon the information about Ginny's episode, please take an educated guess and attempt to fill out a spin of despair worksheet.

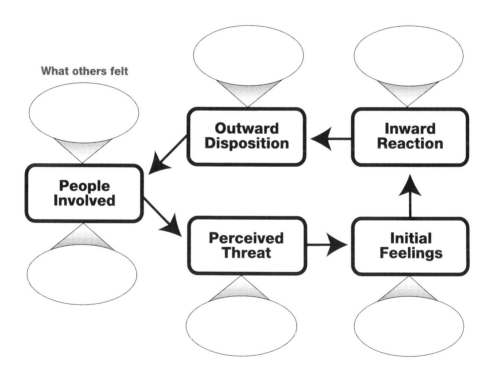

On the next page is Ginny's "Spin of Despair" worksheet. Compare your answers with the one on the next page.

The Spin of Despair:

When someone disagreed with Ginny she felt a perceived threat that she was being unfairly blamed, controlled, cornered, and condescended to. When provoked, Ginny's initial feeling was anger. Her inward reaction was blame. Her outward disposition was fits of anger followed by withdrawal, blame, and condescension toward her husband or others. She was unapproachable, unwilling to listen, resentful, controlling, defensive, and insensitive to those around her. This made her husband and children feel afraid, hurt, and frustrated.

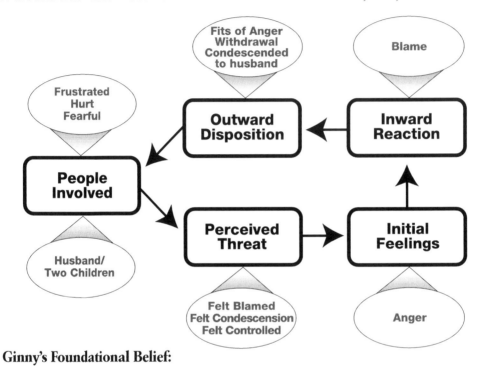

Ginny's Foundational Belief:

Ginny's foundational belief was: In order to be valued and respected, she must be right and in control at all times.

Core Messages:

Ginny's core messages were powerful. Based upon her experience with her parents, she felt her dad treated her mom as a weakling, unable to stand up on her own. He talked down to her, showed her little affection, and controlled the money and all their decisions. She also felt that her dad treated her similarly showing no affection, no attention, and little respect. She was hurt and angry and felt a need to prove herself. She was highly reactive to anyone displaying what she perceived to be condescending or controlling attitudes. Without knowing it, she had developed a vow to never let anyone else treat her like her dad treated her mom and herself. As discussions progressed, it became apparent that Ginny had valid reason to believe that her dad was involved in a lengthy affair behind her mom's back when she was a child, which of course escalated the pain.

Note: It is interesting to note that in Ginny's effort to protect herself from becoming like her mom, she became like her dad in her actions towards others.

Think about it!

1. Before you knew anything about Ginny's background, what were you feeling toward her?

2. Now that you know Ginny's core messages, how does it change your perspective?

3. In the past, what would you have done to help Ginny?

4. Now that you understand the pathway to victory and the power of the cross, what message would you give her?

5. Which of the blessings that result from the cross do you think particularly apply to Ginny's life?

The Cross:

Ginny certainly had an anger issue. It was one that haunted her for years. She knew Christ from the age of 16 and was deeply committed to her church. She had regular devotionals and desperately wished to be different. She had often privately prayed that she could quit displaying her anger but found little relief. Ginny needed Christ. She clearly trusted Him in every way that she knew, but she did not know how to "Take the Gospel to Heart." She, like most, had no idea what was really going on deep inside or how to allow the cross of Christ to minister to her inner heart-cry.

Ginny began trusting Christ for the following promises in her life.

Sonship

Ginny certainly knew that God loved her. But it felt to her more like a far-off love divided by distance and time. Through God's living word Ginny began to experience God's love. This love was compelling and she began to respond very personally back to God through prayer and hunger for His word. For the first time she felt empowered to express emotion to God, truly knowing that he was deeply interested in her and loved her unconditionally. She knew that her outward emotions were a result of sin on her part, which she readily confessed to God and others. She realized she was a beloved daughter of the King; that He danced over her and adored her; that Christ intensely loved her and gave himself for her; that He would always be faithful to her. For the first time in Ginny's life she became secure in Him. She confessed her sin of self-protectiveness and trusted she was in the secure in arms of Christ. She experienced the Abba (daddy) that she had always wanted.

Sanctification/ Created with Purpose

Ginny experienced the peace, hope, and significance that came from knowing that Christ was committed to her sanctification and also created her with specific purpose. She no longer had to perform or try to earn respect. She realized she could rest in His promise to finish His good work in her.

Response to People

Over time Ginny grew from a place of insecurity to confidence around others. She was able to recognize the warning signs when she was falling victim to her fleshly beliefs. When she felt on edge, she learned to quickly deal with any feelings before they exploded within her. She began to take thoughts captive for Christ. She went from feeling at risk around others to feeling secure and purposeful. Her relationship with her husband took on a whole new life. She would later share that she literally viewed him through the blessing of new eyes…she once was blind, but now could see. Does Ginny ever stumble and fall? Of course she does. But it is different. God has given her humility and insight into her need for Him and meets her at her point of need.

Response to God

God had the answer for Ginny's yearning for a loving father. He is the "Abba" Father, you know! At first she was defeated, but in the hands of a restorative God, she experienced Christ-centered brokenness and a contrite heart. He met her with a deep abiding love that set Ginny free. Ginny's response was what you would expect from a girl who had finally met true love. She could not get enough of Him. She was hungry for time and depth of relationship. Ginny continues to learn how to cling to Christ. She knows what it means to "Take the Gospel to Heart."

1. What are several insights that you can gain from Ginny's story?

How can you apply these insights to your life?

Identifying Foundational Beliefs Worksheet

Definition: Foundational Beliefs are fleshly (values) standards invoked by someone on themselves by which they measure their self-worth. To identify potential foundational beliefs, please answer the following questions.

Ginny's Worksheet

1. My "initial feeling" was...

   <u>Anger</u>   Fear   Hurt

2. My "inward reaction" was...

   <u>Blame</u>   Shame   Denial   Medicate

3. The experience made me feel... (circle any that apply)

Misunderstood	Incompetent	Unsafe	Unloved	Used
<u>Disrespected</u>	Unfairly treated	Not accepted	Belittled	<u>Accused</u>
Ridiculed	Unsuccessful	Insignificant	<u>Shamed</u>	<u>Blamed</u>
Insecure	<u>Devalued</u>	Loss of control	Talked down to	Immature
Unappreciated	Unheard	Afraid	Ignored	Left out
Embarrassed	Foolish	<u>Condescended to</u>	Unworthy	Unhappy
Condemned	Unworthy	Stupid	Unpopular	Reputation threatened
Worthless	Abused			

4. What did you feel the experience was saying or insinuating about you personally?
(Maybe the same answer you circled in question #3)

The experience made me feel I *have little value.*
(ex. I have little value/ I am a failure/ I am unlovable/ I am incompetent/ I don't deserve respect/ I am insignificant)

5. One of the identifiable characteristics of foundational belief is consistency. Have you experienced the feelings communicated in answer #4 before?

   ■ Yes   ☐ No   How Often?   ☐ Seldom   ☐ Regular   ■ Frequently

6. What was the desired value you felt denied you in question #4?
(Discovered usually by considering the opposite of answer for question 4)

Desired Value: *Feel Valued and Respected*
(ex. Valued/ Successful/ Loved/ Competent/ Respected/ In Control/ Significant)

7. Based on the answer #6 (Desired Value), please fill in the blanks.

I must be	*Right and in control*	**in order to**	*Feel Valued and Respected* (Desired Value)
When	*I perceive my husband as directive or condescending*	**it especially makes me feel**	*feel reactive anger resulting from feeling devalued and disrespected* (Answer from #4)

Foundational Belief...

I feel I am   *valued and respected*   when   *I am right and in control* .
                (Desired Value)

Sample Answers:
	I am right	I am in charge	The plan is fail-safe	Things go perfectly
	I am admired	No negative feedback	Things stay the same	I am in the inner circle
No one talks about me	I am the best	People are pleased	I get the attention	I am not questioned
Know everything going on	I am in control	There is peace	Fully competent	I get the credit

Ginny's Worksheet

Take the Gospel to Heart

1 People Involved — Husband and two children

2 Perceived Threat(s) — Felt blamed
Felt controlled
Felt condescension

3 Initial Feeling — Anger

4 Inward Reaction — Blame

5 Outward Disposition — Fits of Anger/ Withdrawal/ Embattlement and condescension to my husband

6 Foundational Beliefs

I feel I am _valued and respected_ when _I am right and in control_.

7 Core Messages

From	Message	Feeling Response
1 Dad and Mom	Dad treats mom as though she is weak and unable to stand up on her own. He talks down to her, shows little affection, controls the money and their decisions. Dad aslo treats me with little affection, no attention, and shows little respect.	Anger Hurt Protective Need to prove myself

8 ✝ The Cross

The Promise	New Belief **9**	New Attitude **10**
1 Sonship	God is madly in love with me. This love is unconditional. His love is demonstrated with affection and interest.	I am dearly loved. I feel special and appreciated. I don't need to fight for love. Feel more secure.
2 Sanctified, Adopted, Created with Purpose	God is busy at work in me sanctifying me and using me to make a difference for His Kingdom	God has a very specific and important place for me to make a difference for His glory

11 Response to People — Feel more secure around others. Able to recognize reaction to my past with my dad and isolate it for what it is and deal with it with God preventing anger outburst and frustration with others.

12 Response to God — I know God's great love for me! I have a new sense of hope and encouragement from Him and desire to fellowship with Him.

Case Study 2

Cory

Age: 29

Family Status: Married for six years/ One child age 4

Work Status: Pastor

Other: Christian since age 19

Episode:

One evening, while returning from an out-of-town speaking engagement, Cory experienced overwhelming lustful thoughts. You would think that after a couple of days of serving as a keynote speaker at a Christian conference there would be nothing further from his mind. He continued to dwell on mental pornography and found himself beginning to adventure in his mind toward the idea of stopping at a roadside strip bar that he knew was not far down the road, but a long way from home. He had never done anything like this before, but any sane reasoning was blocked by intense feelings of excitement. He exited the interstate and pulled into the parking lot of the strip bar. With his heart furiously racing he entered the night spot. The initial thrill quickly dissipated into significant guilt. A few minutes later he exited the strip bar distressed and aware that he had gone over the edge.

Cory had struggled with internet pornography from the time he was 12. At 19 he came into a relationship with Christ and was sure that this habit would be the first to go. There was a temporary reprieve but when it returned it came on fast and furious. He managed his issues through hope that came from temporary sobriety and justification. His wife was totally clueless to his struggle.

This experience with the strip bar scared Cory. He found himself entangled in the secret world of pornography and crossing over the line into behavior that could devastate his life and family. On the inside it had already taken a critical toll. On the way home that evening he shamefully wished that the event had never taken place. He wondered how something so dirty, spiritually debilitating, endangering, and embarrassing could become so mind consuming, fascinating, and alluring. He tried to justify how he could keep this event from others with a private commitment to never do it again. But deep inside he knew that the secret element of this indiscretion was a major enabling factor.

The next afternoon he sat down with his wife and shared for the first time his story and the event that had taken place the night before. It was painful and put into motion fear, hurt, and initial conflict with his wife. Ultimately, though, this honest confession placed in action a series of restorative events that served to turn Cory's heart completely to Christ and rescue him from impending doom. Cory did come under the restorative discipline of his church and ultimately lost his job as a result of honest confession to church leadership. Along with the painful job loss Cory experienced a supportive heart of Christ-centered restoration, counsel, and accountability from church leaders.

The Spin of Despair:

The Spin of Despair diagram looks a bit different when relating to "at risk" issues. "Temptation" has taken the place of "Perceived Threat." Please look at the diagram with me.

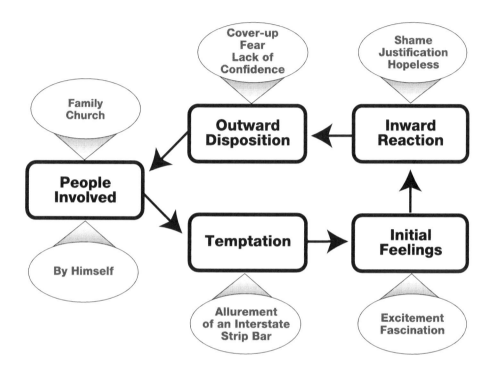

The temptation was the allurement of a strip bar along the Interstate highway. He was pre-occupied with initial feelings of excitement and fascination. It was also a form of escape for Cory. His inward reaction after falling to the temptation was shame. His typical outward disposition was cover-up, lack of confidence, and justification.

This most recent experience, along with other minor ones, always yielded feelings of insecurity, embarrassment, fear, shame, and the anxiety that his reputation, family, and job were threatened. In the past Cory tried to manage his sinful indiscretions through temporary periods of sobriety, living in denial of the dangers by simply writing them off as "what guys deal with," or justifying his behavior by comparing himself to others with seemingly more serious behavior. Outwardly Cory was unable to live authentically. He experienced fear and knew he was a hypocrite. His life, family, and ministry were taking a major hit.

Initially, at the end of each episode, Cory would experience great remorse and recommitment to God. But over time, this remorse and recommitment gave way to a sense of numbness and futility. This lifestyle served to make Cory feel he was a failure and hopeless. He settled into a lifestyle that accepted the spin of despair as the norm.

 Think about it!

1. Besides the area of lust, what are other habitual areas that can yield high levels of challenge to the believer?

2. Cory tried to manage his indiscretions through temporary periods of sobriety, denial, or justification of his behavior compared to others. Do you see any of these "management skills" in play as you deal with fleshly temptation?

Cory's Foundational Belief:

Cory's foundational belief was: I feel I need sexual fantasy to medicate my need for emotional connection.

Core Messages:

Cory experienced an upbringing that met all his physical needs. It was also filled with strong moral teaching and high academic standards. He described his family as the family on the run. They were always doing. Cory never experienced emotional connection with either of his parents. While they encouraged him toward success and provided for his needs, he never remembers any discussions about feelings. He never recalls his parents working through emotional issues. While having a high appreciation for his parent's intentions to meet his physical and academic needs, he realized that he never experienced or learned how to emotionally relate with them or others. Cory recalls loneliness and fear as a child and teen. Early in adolescence he came into contact with friends who shared with him his first taste of Internet pornography. It wasn't long before pornography engulfed Cory. Cory was experiencing both physical and emotional pleasure serving to medicate his loneliness and fear.

 Think about it!

1. Before you knew anything about Cory's background, what were your feelings toward him?

2. Now that you know Cory's core messages, how does it change your perspective?

3. Before you began this study, what would you have told Cory to help him?

4. Now that you understand the pathway to victory and the power of the cross, what message would you give him?

5. Which of the blessings that result from the cross do you think particularly apply to Cory's life?

The Cross:

Cory needed the cross. He had been a believer since in college. Except for a few brief times, he had never experienced intimacy with Christ and freedom from habitual sin.

Cory began trusting Christ for the following promises in his life.

Reconciliation and Sonship

For the first time Cory knew was secure in the fact that he is unconditionally loved. He experienced great relief and the loving arms of Christ when he came out of hiding to deal with issues straightforwardly before God. He experienced the forgiving power of the cross for the first time since his conversion experience. Cory had never experienced emotional intimacy with anyone. Through his new understanding of His Abba Father's love for him and the desire to truly know and relate with him, Cory's heart was opened in ways he had never known. He experienced a real emotional connection with God.

Sanctification

Cory realized he is not on his own. The God that saved him through the work of Christ on the cross is the same God that will sanctify him. He is learning dependency in Christ alone. He is battling daily his old habits related to performance. He knows he has all the firepower necessary to win the battles against the flesh. He recognizes that dependency is an active responsibility of seeking and clinging. While the journey has had very painful moments, Cory is now experiencing the riches and fullness of Christ. He is fully aware of his fleshly weakness regarding lust, but Christ has given him great victory. Any time there are temptations, Cory has been quick to confess weakness, communicate vulnerably with accountability partners, and in Christ's power run from temptation.

Response to People

He and his wife now experience an authentic and deeply loving relationship, one that they now recognize was never there before. After a couple of years away from full-time ministry, Cory re-entered the pastorate with a sense of peace and confidence that he had never experienced before. He was back with a new level of understanding of people and their pain, a new authenticity, and a clear dependence upon Christ. In spite of consistent victory, Cory knew the vulnerability of his flesh. He learned to take the gospel to heart daily. He kept close accountability with his wife and a band of brothers. Prior to Cory's new understanding of the work of Christ, he was guarded in relationships. He stayed away from the emotional needs of others including his family. Now Cory continues to learn to embrace and properly work through his emotions as well as those around him. Doors for relational ministry have broken wide open. He is now an open book. His relationship with his wife is honest and growing. His leadership has a new air of gentleness and mercy. His preaching is clearly centered on the gospel of Christ.

Response to God

Cory lives with a thankful spirit for God's love and forgiveness. He is particularly hungry for an intimate connection with Christ which he has craved for years. He can't share enough about God's fatherly love and interest in his life. Cory continues to learn to cling to Christ. He knows what it means to "Take the Gospel to Heart."

 Think about it!

1. What are several insights that you can gain from Cory's story?

2. How can you apply these insights to your life?

Identifying Foundational Beliefs Worksheet
At-Risk Behavioral Worksheet

> Definition: Foundational Beliefs are fleshly (values) standards invoked by someone on themselves by which they measure their self-worth. To identify potential foundational beliefs, please answer the following questions.

Cory's Worksheet

1. My "initial motivation" was...

    <u>Excitement</u>   Escape   Relief

2. My "inward reaction" was...

    Blame   <u>Shame</u>   Denial   Medicate

3. The experience made me feel... (circle any that apply)

Misunderstood	Incompetent	Unsafe	Unloved	Used
Disrespected	Unfairly treated	Not accepted	Belittled	Accused
Ridiculed	Unsuccessful	Insignificant	<u>Shamed</u>	Blamed
<u>Insecure</u>	Devalued	Loss of control	Talked down to	Immature
Unappreciated	Unheard	<u>Afraid</u>	Ignored	Left out
<u>Embarrassed</u>	Foolish	Condescended to	Unworthy	Unhappy
Condemned	<u>Unworthy</u>	Stupid	Unpopular	<u>Reputation threatened</u>
<u>Worthless</u>	Abused			

4. What did you feel the experience was saying or insinuating about you personally?
(Maybe the same answer you circled in question #3)

The experience made me feel I *am a failure and hopeless.*

(ex. I have little value/ I am a failure/ I am unlovable/ I am incompetent/ I don't deserve respect/ I am insignificant)

5. One of the identifiable characteristics of foundational belief is consistency. Have you experienced the feelings communicated in answer #4 before?

    ■ Yes ☐ No   How Often?   ☐ Seldom ☐ Regular ■ Frequently

6. What was the perceived need you were trying to meet?
Perceived Need:

7. What was the real need (value desired) you were trying to meet?

8. Based on the answer #7 (Real Need), please fill in the blanks.

I must be	*Involved with lustful thought and activities*	in order to	*Feel a sense of fulfillment and happiness*
When	*I chase out after a fleshly high*	I am really seeking	*Emotional connection and love*

Foundational Belief...
I feel I am medicating my need for <u>*emotional connection*</u> when <u>*I am chasing sexual fantasy*</u>.

(Real Need/Value Desired)

Sample Answers:

	I am right	I am in charge	The plan is fail-safe	Things go perfectly
	I am admired	No negative feedback	Things stay the same	I am in the inner circle
No one talks about me	I am the best	People are pleased	I get the attention	I am not questioned
Know everything going on	I am in control	There is peace	Fully competent	I get the credit

Cory's Worksheet At-Risk Behavioral Worksheet

Take the Gospel to Heart

1 Situational Description — Continual battle with internet pornography / recently visited a strip bar

2 Losses or Potential Losses — Out of control fleshly chase
Could have lost my reputation
Could have lost my wife
Lost my job

3 Initial Motivation — Excitement and Escape

4 Initial Response — Fear and Reality Check / Shame

5 Perceived Need — Need to chase a high / Desiring sexual fulfillment / Conquering / Fantasy

Real Need (Desired Value) — Emotional connection...
deep inside these indiscretions came from a deeper need to know and experience emotional love and connection as well as a physical high that created a sense of pleasure and escape.

6 Foundational Belief

I feel I am medicating my need for _emotional connection_ when _I am chasing sexual fantasy_.

7 Core Messages

From	Message	Feeling Response
1 Parents	Little emotional connection from either parent. Mostly just did life and ignored anything personal or feelings based.	No validation of feelings. Felt unloved. Felt disconnected.

8 ✝ The Cross

The Promise	New Belief **9**	New Attitude **10**
1 Reconciled and Sonship	I am secure in the fact that I am unconditionally loved and fully sought after by God	It is great to come out of hiding and deal with those issues straightforwardly before God. Thank God for the cross! I have a new emotional connection to God.
2 Sanctification	I am not my own. God who saved me will sanctify me. He has all the firepower necessary to win these battles. I must actively pursue and cling to Him.	Feel excited and hopeful. Can see God greatly at work in me. For the first time I feel real around others and empowered by God with strength and victory over sin.

11 Response to People — I am more open than ever. No longer hiding anything. Feel very validated by my wife and family. Experiencing real love from others as they stand with me through the challenges.

12 Response to God — Have repented of sin. So excited about God's unconditional love for me and personal interest in every area of my life.

Notes

Made in the USA
Charleston, SC
17 August 2013